Social Networking for Genealogists

The purchase of this item was made possible by a generous grant received from

Social

Networking

for Genealogists

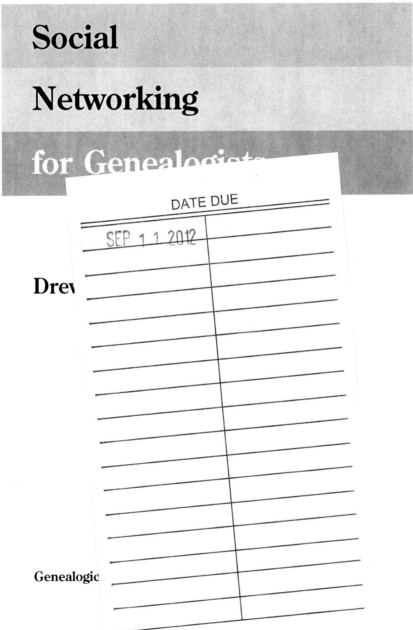

Drew

Genealogic

Published by Genealogical Publishing Company
3600 Clipper Mill Rd., Suite 260
Baltimore, Maryland 21211-1953
Library of Congress Catalogue Card Number 2009921403
ISBN 978-0-8063-1795-3
Made in the United States of America

Contents

Chapter 1:
Introduction

What is social networking, and what does it mean for genealogists and their research methods?

social networking (noun): A way of using online resources and services to create and maintain a community of individuals who share a common interest

What is social networking?

If we weren't talking about computers or the World Wide Web, the term "social networking" might bring to mind the idea of joining clubs, attending parties, engaging in office politics, or volunteering for a community project. Human beings are social animals, and we have a long history of building relationships with others, making new friends, and strengthening existing ties. We enjoy activities that put us in contact with others who share our interests: sporting and recreational events, cultural events, political rallies, religious services, educational lectures, conventions, shopping trips . . . the list goes on. We value the existence of special places that make these kinds of social networking possible: stadiums, auditoriums, houses of worship, classrooms, convention centers, shopping malls. Within these places, we can find those who share our interests and who enjoy talking with us about them. If these places did not exist, we would feel more isolated and cut off from the rest of society.

What happens when computer technology advances to a point where there are "virtual" places people "can go" in order to engage in social networking? We "go" to our electronic mailbox as if it were the physical mailbox in front of our home. We "go" to a website as if it were a store or club-house. Although computer networks date back to the late 1960s, and the Web itself to the early 1990s, it has been only in the past decade that we've seen an explosion of social networking sites and services appear online, and even more recently that a large number of these have been designed specifically for genealogists.

This book is about the type of social networking made possible by the development of international computer networks; availability of net-work access to most homes (especially broadband access); creation of web-sites dedicated to particular kinds of networking (posting photos, viewing and commenting on videos, seeing what books friends have in their librar-ies, etc.); and ease of participating in these sites without having to be a computer expert.

More to the point, this book is intended to identify those kinds of social networking sites and services that will be of the most interest to ge-nealogists. After all, most social networking sites were never developed with genealogists in mind (although this book will certainly discuss those sites that were). There are so many different sites that it can be confusing and overwhelming to explore them.

Beginning with Chapter 4, this book devotes a chapter to each kind of social networking site that might prove useful as part of genealogical re-search. In each chapter, you'll learn a little bit about the history of that kind of site, and you'll be given details about some of the best sites to explore. At the end of each chapter is a handy to-do list that will allow you to follow up on what you've learned in the chapter.

Chapters 2 and 3 cover the basic social networking concepts of RSS and tags. Because these concepts will appear again and again in later chap-ters, it is recommended that you start with these chapters so that you will understand those concepts when you encounter them later.

Genealogists and social networking

When you first suggest to a genealogist that he or she should get in-volved with social networking, you might get the reaction, "I'm doing fine with my research. Why would I need social networking?" The same kind of argument could have been made about the Web, genealogy software, e-mail, and PCs. Clearly, genealogists have successfully engaged in genea-logical research for centuries without any of these technological tools. Nobody here is arguing that you have to become a social networking user in order to become a successful genealogist.

But genealogists are encouraged to seek out new resources and adopt new tools that may prove to be valuable. If a social networking service makes it easier for you to discover a researcher working on the same line as you, share your research with others, see a photo of an ancestral town or building, locate new genealogy sites of interest, ask another genealogist to do a look-up in a rare reference book, find a useful genealogy how-to video, or work together with other genealogists on a group project, isn't it worth your time to learn about such a service and see if it fits into your interests and research methods?

When you became a genealogist, you undoubtedly learned about places you should go (libraries, archives, courthouses, cemeteries, etc.) and tools you should use (library catalogs, microfilm readers, genealogy software and websites). This book will build upon that by introducing you to new "places" and new tools.

Getting involved with social networking

To get involved with social networking as part of your genealogical research, you might take the following incremental steps:

1. **Read** the chapters of this book that deal with RSS and tags, because those concepts will appear again and again as part of many different kinds of social networking services.

2. **Skim** the remaining chapters to understand the various kinds of social networking services.

3. **Read** the chapters about those kinds of social networking services that are most appealing to you.

4. **Act** on the "getting involved" lists that appear at the end of each chapter.

Chapter 2:
RSS

Keeping up with an ever-changing Web

RSS (noun): A type of computer file format used to communicate to others when a website has changed some of its contents

web feed (noun): A file in RSS (or similar) format that is associated with a particular website and can be read by specialized software

aggregator (noun): A type of software (or online service) designed to access web feeds from many different websites and display the results on a single screen. Also known as a "feed reader"

What is web syndication and why is it needed?

You may be glad to know that "RSS" is one of the few initialisms or acronyms you'll have to learn as part of social networking. In order to understand the concept of RSS, it is not necessary to know what the initialism stands for, but for most of us, it stands for "Really Simple Syndication." But what is "syndication?"

The word "syndication" probably brings to your mind the TV series that originally appeared as part of network broadcasts but are now sold directly to individual TV stations. Or you may be thinking of newspaper cartoonists or columnists whose syndicated cartoons and columns are made available for purchase by individual newspapers. But what does "syndication" mean when we're talking about the Web? In the case of web syndication, the word "syndication" refers to the idea that the new, updated content of a particular website will be made available to specific individuals upon request.

You may have noticed that websites differ from one another a great deal in how often they are updated. Some websites are set up once and never changed again. Or a website may have been set up, updated for a while, and then abandoned, leaving it as it was last updated for many years. Other sites may be updated annually, monthly, weekly, daily, or as frequently as several times an hour. They may be updated regularly or irregularly. And websites may cycle back and forth in terms of being updated frequently and then rarely.

So if there are a large number of websites that have interesting content (which may change at any moment), how are you going to know when any of them has something new? It's impractical and discouraging to visit a long list of sites each day, only to discover that the vast majority of them haven't been changed. What you need is a simple way to monitor lots of different websites and be automatically notified about only those that have been updated. We need a "really simple" way to "syndicate" the updated content of websites to those individuals who want to be kept informed of changes.

Web feeds and RSS

In order for web syndication to work, there has to be a way for the owners of websites to notify others when they have updated their websites, and for the consumers of the information to know when a site of interest has been updated. This is accomplished by the website owner creating a special file known as a "web feed." This file will be in a format readable by specialized software so that it can be turned into a human-readable form for the end user. Because it was desirable that many different websites use the same format for their web feeds, a standard format known as RSS was proposed in 1999. As in many other areas of computing technology, there are now competing file format standards, the two most common being RSS 2.0 and Atom. Fortunately, because of the capabilities of the software that reads and interprets the web feeds, the end user doesn't have to worry about what format the feed is in. To make things here a bit simpler, we'll refer to all web feeds as if they use the RSS format.

Many of the social networking sites in this book offer some sort of web feed in order for users to keep track of new content. A message board will have new messages. A blog will have new entries or new comments on existing entries. A photo sharing site will have new photos or new comments on existing photos. A podcast site will have new episodes. Each of these sites will provide an RSS web feed. When you visit a website that provides an RSS web feed, the link for the feed will usually be identified by a standard logo similar to this:

Or you may encounter an orange rectangle with the word "RSS" in it or some other variation. You may also find multiple feeds for a given website. On a blog, for instance, there may be one feed for the new blog entries and a separate feed for the comments that other individuals post in response to the entries. A site may provide different feeds for different topics or a way to create your own custom feed so that you get notified about only those particular items you're interested in. You'll find more details about this in the later chapters of this book.

Online aggregator service

In order to keep track of all of the web feeds you're interested in, you'll need either specialized software installed on your computer or access to an online service that can be used on any computer connected to the Internet. The specialized software or online service that is designed to subscribe to, manage, and display results from web feeds is known as an "aggregator." Let's look first at an example of a very popular online-based aggregator, and then at a software-based one.

Because of its dominance in many online services (web searching, e-mail, online news, etc.), it should come as no surprise that Google provides a popular and easy-to-use aggregator as one of its suite of free online services. Once you have created a free Google account, you can follow the "Reader" link to access Google Reader, or you can visit the URL www .google.com/reader. Here is a look at a Google Reader screen:

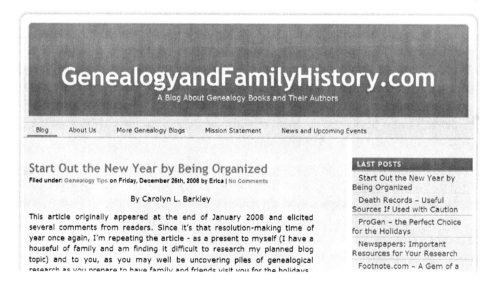

Let's see how we would subscribe to a particular genealogy blog using Google Reader. For this example, I'm interested in a blog called GenealogyandFamilyHistory.com, available at http://www.genealogyand familyhistory.com:

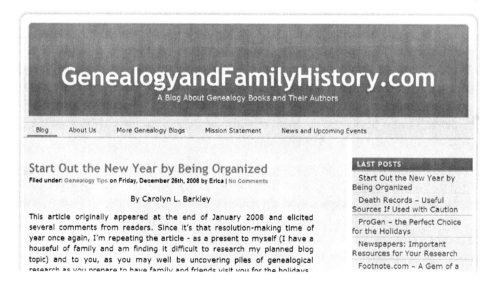

Now that we're at the website, we should look for the RSS logo, an RSS button, or some other link that identifies the web feed for the website. At the bottom of the first page, we find this:

« Previous Entries

GenealogyandFamilyHistory.com is proudly powered by WordPress 2.5.1 and NikyNik Theme
Entries (RSS) and Comments (RSS).

We have a choice of subscribing to the blog's entries or to the comments that others leave in response to the entries. We can go through this process twice and subscribe to both. Let's click on the link for the RSS web feed for the entries:

Subscribe to this feed using   8 Google   ▾

☐ Always use Google to subscribe to feeds.

Subscribe Now

In this case, I'm given an option as to what aggregator I want to use for keeping track of my web feeds. I'll choose Google:

GenealogyandFamilyHistory.com
A Blog About Genealogy Books and Their Authors
http://www.genealogyandfamilyhistory.com/?feed=rss2

Google offers two different ways to keep up-to-date with your favorite sites:

Your Google homepage brings together Google functionality and content from across the web, on a single page.

Google Reader makes it easy to keep up with the latest content from a large number of sites, all on a single reading list.

Add to Google homepage   or   Add to Google Reader

─── Sample ───

─── Sample ───

Google gives me a choice of adding the subscription to my Google home page or to my Google Reader online service. Because I keep track of a large number of web feeds, I'll choose Google Reader:

Because I read websites on many different topics, I assign my web feeds to particular categories. In this case, I'll want to assign the Genealogyand FamilyHistory.com web feed to my "genealogy" category:

After I add GenealogyandFamilyHistory.com to my genealogy folder, the screen will look like this:

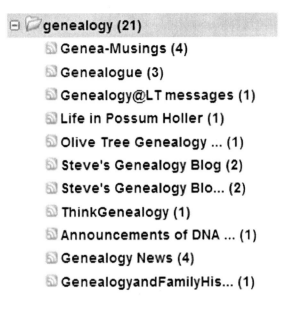

I can also move the items around so that the web feeds appear in whatever order I prefer. By clicking the left-hand menu of my Google Reader screen, I can have Google Reader display all of my items, only those in a particular folder, or only those in a particular web feed.

As I read each item, I can also click on its title to take me directly to the website itself.

Software-based aggregator

The advantage of an online aggregator service is that you have automatic access to it from any computer that is connected to the Internet. If you already have a Google account, then setting up a Google Reader set of web feeds is fast and easy. But if you would prefer to keep your web feed subscriptions locked away on your personal computer, you may feel better with a software solution. In the past, you might have had to look for specialized software that needed to be downloaded, but today aggregator features are already built into the current versions of the most popular web browsers. Let's look at the one already available in Firefox 3:

When I visit the blog GenealogyandFamilyHistory.com, Firefox displays an RSS logo in the far right of the URL:

http://www.genealogyandfamilyhistory.com/

Clicking on the RSS logo gives me this:

Subscribe to 'RSS 2.0'...

Subscribe to 'RSS .92'...

Subscribe to 'Atom 0.3'...

Firefox gives me a choice of which web feed file format I want to use (in case my aggregator software is limited as to which formats it can read). I'll choose the RSS 2.0 format:

Subscribe to this feed using   Google

☐ Always use Google to sub   Live Bookmarks

Microsoft Office Outlook

Choose Application...

Bloglines

My Yahoo

Google

Notice that I'm given the same choices as I had with Google Reader, but this time I'll choose "Live Bookmarks" instead. (But notice that you could even use Microsoft Office Outlook as your software-based aggregator if you wanted to.)

Choosing "Live Bookmarks" brings up the following pop-up window:

As you can see, I have a variety of places I could store the RSS web feed for this website among my other, more typical browser bookmarks. Once I have the website's feed as a Live Bookmark, I can click on it to see a list of the entries:

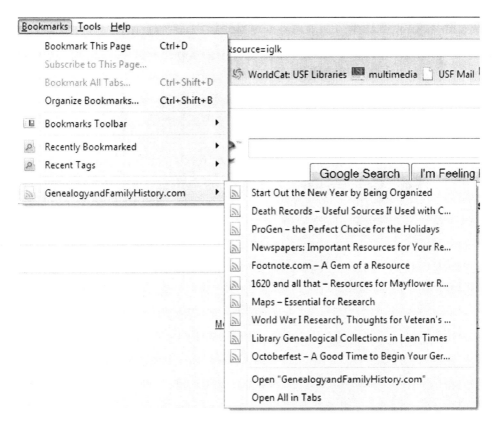

Every 60 minutes, Firefox will check each of your web feeds to see if there are any changes to the entries and will refresh your Live Bookmarks. If you don't want to wait 60 minutes, you can right-click on the name of the Live Bookmark and choose "Reload Live Bookmark."

Final comments

As you read later chapters in this book, you may find it helpful to return here whenever you come across a reference to RSS or web feeds. Using an aggregator will make it easier for you to stay involved with a number of different social networking sites without having to visit each site directly just to see if it has any interesting new content.

Getting involved with RSS

To get involved with RSS as part of your genealogical research, you might take the following incremental steps:

1. **Set up** an account at a free aggregator website, such as Google Reader.

2. **Subscribe** to one or more web feeds by visiting one of the social networking sites discussed later in the book and then clicking on the feed icon or appropriate link.

3. **Read** items of interest from feeds you have subscribed to.

4. **Organize** your feeds into categories.

Chapter 3:
Tags

Everyone gets their own label maker

tag (noun): A word or short phrase used to identify or describe some item of information (such as a textual entry, photograph, or video) in order to make it easier to find later

tag (verb): To assign one or more tags to an item of information

folksonomy (noun): An informal classification system resulting from a large number of people applying tags of their own choosing to items in a repository of information

The problem of applying labels to information

Examine the typical spice rack in a kitchen, and you'll see each small jar labeled to identify which spice is inside each jar. Look at the typical small parts cabinet of drawers in a home workshop, and you'll quickly determine which drawers contain short screws and which drawers contain long ones. Pull open a typical home office genealogical filing cabinet, and you'll see folder after folder, each labeled with a surname, individual name, place name, or some other descriptor for the contents of the folder. We are used to labeling the things we own so that we can quickly find them again.

And if others need to use our spices or our workshop parts, it is unlikely that they will have trouble finding what they need, unless we have used strange terms for the labels or a strange way to arrange the items. Figuring out our organizational scheme for our personal genealogical research might give others some difficulty, but eventually someone could look at what we had done and figure out whether we used a scheme that was alphabetical, geographical, chronological, or some combination of those.

When we place labels on physical objects (such as spice bottles, parts drawers, and filing folders), we are normally limited to only a few words. The same could be said of some kinds of electronic objects. We create file names and folder names on our computers, realizing that we had best use something that will quickly tell us what is in the file or folder. We try to use a few words that tell us what the file or folder is "about." If you've ever looked for a file on your computer before, you'll appreciate the art of good labeling and the woes of finding the file if you gave it a strange name or put it in a folder with a strange name.

Finally, when it comes to organizing electronic information, the typical file-and-folder system has one major problem: The file has a single file name, and the file goes into one particular folder. If you've got a genealogy document describing your great-grandfather Robert King's military service in South Carolina, does the file go into a folder called "Robert King," "military service," or "South Carolina?"

In the kitchen, you will probably have only a few dozen spices. In the home workshop, you will probably have only a few dozen parts drawers. But on your computer, you may have tens or hundreds of thousands of computer files. On the Web, there may be many millions of interesting documents, photos, videos, and other kinds of computer files. What kind of labeling process is going to allow you and others to find information of interest?

What are tags, and how do they help?

A tag is a word or very brief phrase that can be used to describe an item of information, making it easier to locate that same item again later. It differs from the typical file name or file-and-folder system in that you can assign multiple tags to the same item. The genealogical document I described earlier could be tagged with "Robert King," "military service," and "South Carolina." (Note that some tagging systems do not allow you to use tags consisting of more than one word, so in this case I might have to use "RobertKing," "militaryservice," and "SouthCarolina" instead.) This means that I can easily locate the document by remembering just one of the tags that I used to mark it with.

Your first reaction to all of this might be to point out that search engines can already locate documents on your computer or on the Web by searching all of the words they contain. So where is the benefit of tagging over a search engine?

First, unfortunately, a search engine treats all words in the document the same, although you may be able to distinguish those that appear in the title from those that appear elsewhere in the document. This means that if the document refers to my great-grandfather only as "R.B. King," my search for "Robert King" won't find him. And if I search for "South Carolina," I may get a large number of irrelevant documents that happen to mention "South Carolina" somewhere in the text even though the document isn't really about South Carolina.

Second, a search engine cannot easily identify the contents of a photo, video, or audio file, apart from any attached file name. Tagging can be used to provide the text needed to describe and identify audiovisual material.

Let's look at some examples of tagging used in a few social networking sites.

Tagging on a message board

Here's an example taken from Ancestry.com's Message Boards:

🖼 Holladay Descendants

> Replies: 10
>
> ▣ **Re: Holladay Descendants**
>
> 🖼 Andrew Smith 🌟 (View posts)   Posted: 16 Oct 2008 2:09PM
> Classification: Query
> Surnames: Holladay, Corbett
>
> According to the 1900, 1910, and 1920 censuses, Joseph Benjamin Holladay and his wife, Eula Lee Corbett, had the following 8 children:
>
> daughter Lottie L., born August 1887
> son John Benjamin, born September 1890
> son Olin B., born July 1892
> son Ezra S., born May 1894
> daughter Hattie L., born August 1897
> daughter Huldy Josephine, born October 1899
> daughter Mary/May? Camilla, born about 1902
> daughter Ellis? Isabella, born about 1907
>
>   Reply   Report Abuse   Print

Notice that the title of the message "Holladay Descendants" wouldn't be enough to tell you that the message was about a particular Holladay who had married a Corbett. Ancestry.com's Message Boards provide a tag-like feature for the message board poster to identify the relevant surnames, which you see listed near the top of the message. This feature makes it easier to locate messages of interest, especially when the research surname might be confused with an ordinary English word, such as "King" or "Brown."

Tagging on a blog

Here's an example from Stephen J. Danko's blog (*Steve's Genealogy Blog*):

He signed the Petition on 22 Apr 1935 at Worcester;

»

His Certificate of Arrival was No. 1 150638;

»

His Petition was signed by W. A. Hopkins, Deputy Clerk for William C. Brown, Clerk of the Superior Court;

»

The Petition was received by the U.S. Immigration and Naturalization Service on 14 Jul 1937.

This document provides some valuable information beyond that of Damian Niedzialkowski's efforts to become a United States citizen. I now have additional information about Damian's birth, his wife, his marriage, and his daughter. With this information, I hope to find Damian's marriage record in Massachusetts and, consequently, discover the names of his parents. Perhaps, with this information, I can learn if and how he is connected to my own Niedzialkowski family.

Written for the Carnival of Eastern European Genealogy.

Copyright © 2008 by Stephen J. Danko

Posted in Daily Journal, Naturalization, Niedzialkowski | No Comments »

» Land Records (3)
» Landry (11)
» LeBlanc (19)
» Letters (1)
» Lithuania (21)
» Locations (1)
» Magazines (1)
» Maps (14)
» Markiewicz (25)
» Marriage Indexes (1)
» Marriage Records (31)
» Marriage Records (23)
» Martin (11)
» McGinn (3)
» Message Boards (3)
» Methodology (11)
» Milewski (29)
» Military Records (19)
» Naturalization (21)
» NEHGS (3)
» New Brunswick (3)
» Newspapers (6)
» Niedzialkowski (184)

At the end of the blog entry is a list of tags which Steve Danko has assigned to this particular entry (in this example, "Daily Journal," "Naturalization," and "Niedzialkowski"). These tags appear as "Categories" in a right-hand menu on each page of the blog, making it easy to find only those blog entries tagged as "Naturalization" or "Niedzialkowski," regardless of what actual words may appear in the text of the blog entry.

Tagging on a photo/video sharing site

As mentioned earlier, tagging becomes very important on a site that features non-textual information, such as sites that feature photos, videos, or audio files. Let's look at the most popular example, the photo sharing site known as Flickr:

George and Lizzie Martin family of Newberry, SC

Share This

Uploaded on December 23, 2008
by drewsmithfl

drewsmithfl's photostream

You are at the first photo.   You are at the last photo.   1 upload

browse

This photo also belongs to

Martin (Set)

You are at the first photo.   You are at the last photo.   1 item

browse

Tags

martin
waller
edna
ernest
virginia
ansel
cleo
lizzie
george
corinne

Add your comment

In this example, a family photo has been uploaded to the Flickr photo sharing website. While the title of the photo gives a general description as to who is represented in the photo, the tags on the right have been added in order to supply the first names of everyone in the photo. Additional tags—such as a year or a street address—could be added.

Pros and cons of tagging

Tags provide a fast and easy way to assign labels to shared information, making it possible for a very large number of people to search among large amounts of shared information in order to discover items of interest. Imagine how handy it is to search and find the right message from among millions of messages on a message board, the right blog posting from among hundreds of postings in a particular blog, or the right photo from among millions of photos on a photo sharing website.

But the advantages of tagging (that it is quick and easy) are also its disadvantages. Because tagging can be done quickly, it is easy for a tagger to misspell a word or assign the wrong word to an item. And different taggers may make different choices for the same item. One person may tag a document as "Robert King," another person may tag it as "R.B. King," and a third person may tag it as "Robert B. King." Because there is no top-down authority to set the rules for tagging, tags may be misspelled, inconsistent, and idiosyncratic. One person may go into great detail using a lot of tags, while another person may find it time-consuming and only bother to assign one or two tags.

But what is the alternative? Other kinds of classification systems that we may encounter, such as those used in a public library or academic library catalog, are designed and implemented by highly trained professionals, who must spend a great deal of time on each item in order to be careful that the best possible "tags" are assigned to each library item. And because these professional systems are coordinated among many tens of thousands of librarians, they are relatively slow to change and adopt new terms as needed. Librarians may not yet have gained the expertise in a quickly changing discipline of knowledge in order to know when they need to change or further develop the classification system.

Tagging, meanwhile, is well designed to fit the world of the Web and specifically of social networking sites. With tagging performed by interested, experienced enthusiasts and hobbyists, new terms can be added as needed, and the sheer size of the hobbyist population can keep up with the explosive number of message board postings, blog entries, photos, and videos. In many cases, the tagger will be the person who created the information in the first place, meaning that the tagger is in the best position to describe and identify what the information is.

The resulting classification system, built from the ground up, is a "folksonomy." Folksonomies are a kind of informal classification system that comes into existence simply by the efforts of individuals tagging their own information (or that of others). As you visit various social networking sites, take notice of how tagging is used.

Getting involved with tags

To get involved with tags as part of your genealogical research, you might take the following incremental steps:

1. **Search** a social networking site that uses tags and see what kinds of results you get.

2. **Assign** your own tags to an item of interest, such as a photo or video.

Chapter 4:
Message boards and mailing lists

An electronic message in a bottle

message board (noun): A website or similar location that allows individuals to compose and publish messages that can be read by others at the same site

mailing list (noun): A service that allows individuals to compose and send e-mail messages that can be received and read by others interested in the same topic

post (verb): To publish a message on a message board or send a message to a mailing list

poster (noun): One who posts

subscribe (verb): To add the RSS web feed for a particular message board to your aggregator, or to arrange for your e-mail address to automatically receive all messages sent to a particular mailing list

GenForum

For the modern genealogist, the primary genealogy message boards of interest are GenForum (hosted at genforum.genealogy.com) and the Ancestry.com Message Boards (hosted at boards.ancestry.com). GenForum, which was founded in July 1997, became a service of The Generations Network (TGN) in 2003, when TGN purchased Genealogy.com. Unfortunately, since the purchase, additional social networking features have not been added to GenForum in favor of TGN's other genealogy message board property, the Ancestry.com Message Boards. Even so, the GenForum boards continue to be used by genealogists. Here is a shot of GenForum's home page:

At one time a number of years ago, GenForum had a feature on its home page that allowed the user to search across all of the message boards at the same time to attempt to locate a word (such as a surname or place). Unfortunately, this feature was removed and there appear to be no plans to add it back. As a workaround, users may be able to use Google to locate messages of interest in GenForum. For instance, a search for the surname "Bodie" across all of the GenForum boards could be performed in Google by using the following search terms:

site:genforum.com bodie

Ancestry.com Message Boards—searching for a message

Because TGN has added a number of social networking features in the past few years to its Ancestry.com Message Boards, let's devote the rest of our discussion of genealogy message boards to exploring the Ancestry .com Message Boards. Let's start at the home page:

The home page of the Ancestry.com Message Boards provides a way to search all of its 17 million posts at the same time. As you might imagine, a search for a common name or place might result in a very large, essentially unusable number of hits. But we can remedy that problem by using the link to Advanced Search:

Message Boards

You are here: Message Boards > Advanced Search

Advanced Search

Tip: Visit the Board FAQ for tips on how to make your searches more effective.

Name or Keyword		
Subject of Message		
Author of Message		
Last Name (surname)		☐ Use Soundex
Message Classification	All ▾	
Posted Within	Anytime ▾	

Search

Are the advanced search features useful? Some are clearly more useful than others. For instance, the "Name or Keyword" search is already on the basic search screen, so it's only going to be useful when you combine it with one of the other search features. The "Subject of Message" feature will be helpful only if the author (sometimes referred to as a "poster") of the message used a descriptive subject line. The "Author of Message" feature is likely to be most useful if you are trying to relocate a message that you have seen previously and you remember the name of the person who posted it.

The "Last Name (surname)" feature, which I previously described in Chapter 3, is useful for searching because it limits your hits to those messages where the author explicitly listed the relevant surnames from the message. This helps to avoid large numbers of hits when the surname happens to match a common English word or common first name. However, researchers should not become too dependent on this feature. Messages that were posted before this feature became available won't have any surname tags on them, and authors are not required to add surname tags to their messages (and so they may not bother). The "Soundex" checkbox allows the searcher to expand the search for surnames with the same Soundex codes, making it easier to find messages where the surnames have spelling variations.

The "Message Classification" feature exploits another kind of tag that authors of the Ancestry.com Message Boards can use. When an author posts a message, the author can choose from one of the following categories for the message: Query (which is the default value), Bible, Biography, Birth, Cemetery, Census, Death, Deed, Immigration, Lookup, Marriage, Military, Obituary, Pension, Will, Other. Messages posted prior to the existence of this feature will automatically have the default tag "Query" (regardless of their contents), and for newer messages authors may not bother to change the default value of "Query" to a more specific classification.

The "Posted Within" feature can be very useful if a researcher visits the Ancestry.com Message Boards on a regular basis. This feature makes it possible to limit the search to messages posted within a certain time frame prior to the day of the search: 1 Day, 3 Days, 1 Week, 1 Month, 6 Months, 1 Year. This means that the researcher can perform an exhaustive search, mark a date on the calendar for some time in the future (say, one year), and return on that future date to search for and view only those messages that have been added since the time of the original search.

Ancestry.com Message Boards—locating a particular board of interest

Another way to discover messages of interest (instead of doing a global search) is to visit a board dedicated to a particular surname, place, or other genealogy-related topic. If you have a particular surname, place name (such as country, state, or county), or topic in mind, you can search for a relevant board:

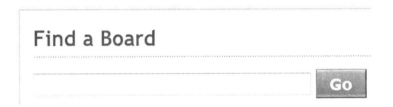

Another option is to browse for a board by using one of the sets of links listed below the "Find a Board" search box. For instance, you can look for a board for a particular surname (this may work better than using the "Find a Board" search box if you're unsure as to what spelling of the surname is being used for the board. Many surname-related genealogy message boards may cover two or more spelling variations for the surname, but the board can be listed only under one particular surname in the directory:

SURNAMES

A B C D E F G H I J K L M N O P Q R S T U V W X Y Z

Begin your searching by clicking on the first letter of the surname. On the next screen, choose the first two letters of the surname, and on the final screen, choose the first three letters of the surname. At this point, you'll be presented with a list of all surname message boards that start with those three letters. For instance, if I am looking for all surname message boards that might be relevant to the surname "Boddie," I would click on the links until I saw this screen:

Bod...

Viewing 1 - 100 of **102** | Next

Board	Threads	Messages	Last Post
Bod	1	1	25 Apr 2000
Boda	12	29	2 Sep 2008
Bodahelyi	0	0	
Bodal	2	3	18 Oct 2002
Bodamer	7	30	30 Aug 2008
Bodard	1	1	18 Aug 2001
Bodart	4	7	6 Apr 2007
Bodda	1	5	17 Jun 2007
Boddan	2	2	8 Dec 2008
Bodde	2	7	15 Dec 2006
Boddeker	1	4	5 Nov 2006
Bodden	5	22	1 Oct 2008
Boddicker	3	9	6 Jan 2008
Boddie	61	190	26 Dec 2008

I would notice that there's a relatively active board for "Boddie," but also a board for "Bodde." Further down the screen I would also eventually discover boards for "Boddy," "Bodie," and "Body," among others.

In some cases, I may be interested in discussing a particular geographic area with other researchers instead of a surname. You can also browse for a board based upon its geographic location:

LOCALITIES CATEGORIES

Category	Sub-Categories	Boards
Australia	8	2
Canada	14	2
United Kingdom and Ireland	6	1
United States	2	1
Western Europe	14	0
>> More Localities Categories		

By clicking through the links, I could eventually end up in a specific county of interest (in this example, for a county in South Carolina):

Message Boards

You are here: Message Boards > Localities > North America > United States > States > South Carolina > **Counties**

Names or Keywords

Search Advanced Search

◉ All Boards ○ Counties - Family History & Genealogy Message Boards

🗁 Counties
☆ Add Category to Favorites

COUNTIES BOARDS

Board	Threads	Messages	Last Post
Abbeville	1075	2623	29 Dec 2008
Aiken	575	1165	27 Dec 2008
Allendale	60	92	14 Dec 2008
Anderson	1904	4448	31 Dec 2008 11:32AM

Finally, you can locate message boards that discuss topics other than surnames and places, such as genealogy software or types of records. These boards can be browsed:

TOPICS CATEGORIES

Category	Sub-Categories	Boards
🗁 Cemeteries & Tombstones	7	2
🗁 Genealogy Software	0	16
🗁 Immigration and Emigration	6	8
🗁 Military	13	8
🗁 Research Resources	5	16
>> More Topics Categories		

Ancestry.com Message Boards—searching, browsing, and reading a particular board

Once you have reached a particular board of interest, you may notice that you can search just that one board for what you are interested in:

Names or Keywords

Search Advanced Search

◉ All Boards ○ Boddie - Family History & Genealogy Message Board

(This also works for searching all boards listed within a particular category, if you are on the category screen.)

Below the search box for a specific board is the list of subject lines of each thread, the authors of the original messages in each thread, the number of replies to the original message, and the most recent date that a message was posted to each thread. These threads will be listed in order, starting with the thread that has the most recent message posted to it:

🎲 Boddie			Subscribe to RSS
📝 Begin New Thread		Threads: 61 - Messages: 190	
Thread	**Author**	**Replies**	**Last Post**
Boddie Family - Raleigh, NC	👤 dsarcia1	0	26 Dec 2008
BODDIE Robert B and Elixabeth P	👤 t42Moore	0	4 Dec 2008
BODDY and families married into in the USA and England	👤 PatriciaTharp	11	27 Oct 2008
Chandler Jefferson and Velma Vernice Cupples(when and where married)	Lauren Ashton...	1	31 Aug 2008
Boddie/Stevens connection?	H. Stevens	4	5 Aug 2008
Ola Virginia Boddie/Alabama	👤 lissap1955	3	17 Jun 2008
Richard Boddie	👤 lastonestandi...	0	12 Jun 2008
Mary C. Boddie b. abt 1895 VA m. Job Padgett	BeckyBrown53	1	23 Mar 2008

Note that some authors have a silhouette icon to the left of their names, while others do not. The icon indicates whether or not the author has a "profile," a common feature on social networking sites. Profiles are used to provide personal information about the author. In the case of Ancestry.com, many different kinds of information may appear in the user's profile. Here is the top portion of my own Ancestry.com profile:

Andrew Smith
Tampa, Florida, USA

Drew Smith is the Information literacy librarian at the University of South Florida (USF) Tampa Library. He has been actively pursuing genealogical research since 1992.

Edit name, location & intro

Andrew Smith's activity

Member since: 5 Dec 2000
Profile last updated: Today
Last login: Today

Edit photo

Can you help other members?
Tell us if you are able to help other members who may be doing similar research.

Research Interests

Name	Location	Date Range
Bode	upstate South Carolina	1700 -

ABOUT ANDREW SMITH

Personal Info
Member Name: drewsmithcps
Gender: Male
Age Group: 50-59
Education: Graduate Degree
Employment: Full-time
Occupation: Education / Training
Languages: English
Lineage: British Isles, Jewish, Eastern European

Needless to say, any of the information that you choose to put into your profile is purely voluntary, and so you will find many individuals who have very little information in theirs, while other individuals have chosen to share a great many details about themselves. You will see again and again that nearly all social networking sites give you the ability to control nearly all of the personal information about yourself that you choose to share with others.

To read the original message in a thread, click on its subject line. To read the most recent reply, click on the date. Here is an example of a posting I made in reply to another poster's query:

Re: Obituary for Addison R. Bannon, b. 1844 Lawrence Co., PA, d. 1922 Venango Co., PA

Andrew Smith (View posts)   Posted: 23 Aug 2005 4:08PM
Classification: Query

Addison R. Bannon appears in the 1920 Oakland Township, Venango County, PA census in the household of his son, John, and his daughter-in-law (Rebecca?).

In 1910, Addison appears as head of household in the Oakland census with wife Sara and son John.

In both censuses, Addison's father is listed as being born in PA and his mother as being born in OH.

In 1900, Addison appears in North Fayette, Allegheny County, PA with his wife Sarah, and sons John and Frederick. In this census, both of his parents are listed as being born in PA.

In 1880, Addison appears in Rynd Farm, Venango, PA as A. R., with wife Sarah, and children Lillian, Robert, John, and Elizabeth. His parents' birth states match those of the later censuses.

Reply   Report Abuse   Print

Notice that the thumbnail photo appears at the top left because I have my photo in my profile. Clicking on my name will provide a pop-up window with some additional details about me. At this point, we can print out the message if we choose to or reply to it. If a message contains inappropriate subject matter or language, the reader can flag the message for an administrator to review for purposes of deletion.

Ancestry.com Message Boards—keeping up with new messages

One of the traditional drawbacks to using genealogical message board systems is that you never know when a reply has been made to one of your own postings, or you never know if interesting new content has been added to a surname board or other board of potential interest. You would have to remember to visit the board a number of times in the future to see what new messages, if any, have been posted. Fortunately, the Ancestry.com Message Boards provide two ways for you to be automatically notified of these things without having to visit the boards first:

From: **drewsmithtpa**   Not you? Click here.

*Subject:

*Message:

☑ Send me an alert when anyone replies to this thread.

If you leave the "send me an alert" option checked below the bottom of the message, you will receive e-mail whenever someone posts another message to the same thread. This will take place whether someone replies the same day or several years in the future, so you won't have to remember to check back to see if there are any interesting replies.

If you are participating in a message board where a significant percentage of the messages may be of interest to you (such as for a surname you are researching or a county where many of your ancestors resided), you can be notified of any new messages by subscribing to the message board's RSS-format web feed. (See Chapter 2 for a detailed explanation on how to manage web feed subscriptions.)

Yes, each message board that is part of the Ancestry.com Message Boards has its very own web feed! You'll find the RSS subscription link at the top right of the screen:

Mailing lists

Arguably, electronic mailing lists have the barest minimum of social networking features. They do allow individuals who share a common interest to communicate with one another. But because almost all of the interaction takes place via e-mail, they lack such Web-based features as profiles and tagging. I say "almost all," because mailing lists can be archived, and those archives can be made available on the Web for searching and browsing.

There are well over 30,000 electronic mailing lists dedicated to some aspect of genealogical research. The vast majority of those lists can be found in one place: the RootsWeb.com Genealogy Mailing Lists site at lists.rootsweb.ancestry.com. Most genealogy mailing lists not hosted by RootsWeb are found on Yahoo! Groups (a site that combines features of message boards and mailing lists). For the most exhaustive list of genealogy mailing lists (including those not hosted by RootsWeb), visit:

www.rootsweb.ancestry.com/~jfuller/gen_mail.html

The home page for the RootsWeb mailing lists allows you to locate a particular list of interest, as well as search the archives of all of the lists:

Mailing Lists

Find archived posts to RootsWeb's 30,000 genealogical mailing lists or find and subscribe to a list.

> ⓘ Looking for the old Mailing Lists home page? You can still find it by selecting "Browse mailing lists" under the "Find a mailing list" search box or by clicking here.

Search the mailing list archives:

Keyword(s):   Search

Advanced search | Search tips

Find a mailing list:

Keyword(s):   Find

Advanced search | Search tips | Browse mailing lists

If you want to automatically receive all of the messages sent to any particular list, you will want to "subscribe" to the list. When you use the "Find a mailing list" function to locate a list of interest, you will reach a screen that will provide instructions on how to subscribe to the list.

The downside of subscribing to a mailing list is that you are unlikely to be interested in every message posted to the list, and as a result, you will be receiving a potentially large amount of unwanted e-mail. Fortunately, there is a helpful alternative: Each of the RootsWeb mailing lists is archived on the Web, and each list's archive has its own RSS web feed. You will find the RSS icon at the bottom of the list's archive page:

June 2008 1 messages

July 2008 1 messages

August 2008 4 messages

October 2008 1 messages

November 2008 1 messages

RSS

Note: Many Ancestry.com Message Boards are "gatewayed" to the corresponding RootsWeb mailing list. For example, any message posted on the message board for the "Pitts" surname is automatically e-mailed out to the "Pitts" mailing list. To determine whether or not an Ancestry.com Message Board is gatewayed to a RootsWeb mailing list, visit the message board and look to see whether the icon to the immediate left of the message board name has an envelope as part of the design:

For a gatewayed message board, there is no advantage in subscribing to the RSS web feeds for both the board and the mailing list, because every board message is being automatically included on the mailing list. It is sufficient to subscribe only to the web feed for the mailing list. If the message board is not gatewayed, consider subscribing to the web feeds for both the board and the mailing list, so as not to miss any relevant messages.

Getting involved with message boards and mailing lists

To get involved with message boards and mailing lists as part of your genealogical research, you might take the following incremental steps:

1. **Search** the Ancestry.com Message Boards for the names of individuals, surnames, or places of interest. Repeat the search on GenForum.

2. **Search** the RootsWeb mailing lists for the names of individuals, surnames, or places of interest.

3. **Create** a free Ancestry.com account (if you do not already have one).

4. **Subscribe** to an RSS-format web feed for one or more Ancestry.com Message Boards that pertain to your surnames and places of interest.

5. **Subscribe** to one or more RootsWeb mailing lists, either by receiving direct e-mail or by subscribing to the RSS-format web feed for the list's archive.

6. **Reply** to an existing message on the Ancestry.com Message Boards or begin a new thread. Do the same on GenForum.

7. **Reply** to a message that you received from a RootsWeb mailing list or post a new message to one of your subscribed lists.

8. **Edit** your Ancestry.com Public Profile to include whatever information you would like other message board users to know about you.

Chapter 5:
Blogs

Personal research, news, opinions, and the people who comment in response

Blog (noun): A type of website in which new content is automatically displayed at the top of the home page, while older content is displayed further down the page and much older content is archived on other, linked pages

Blog (verb): To maintain a blog

Blogger: A person who blogs

Introduction

When the World Wide Web first came into existence, it was designed around the idea of individual websites, each consisting of one or more web pages, with the ability to link from text on one page to text on another. Within a few years, hobbyists learned how to create their own personal websites, but there was a learning curve involved. It was usually necessary to learn not only the HTML language in order to create and edit the pages but also additional software, such as FTP, used to upload new pages to the Web and replace them as needed with newer versions. If one wanted to keep fresh content on the top of the home page, one could edit the home page and add the new content to the top, but there was no automatic mechanism to remove older content from the bottom or archive it to other pages for later reference.

Even so, by the mid-1990s, a number of individuals were maintaining websites that fit the definition of a blog. Many of these blogs were based around political or social issues and emphasized news and opinions, while others resembled online diaries, a blow-by-blow record of what the blogger was doing each day. Because of the technical knowledge needed to create and archive websites, the number of people involved in blogging remained fairly small until the release in 1998 and 1999 of several easy-to-use blogging tools, such as LiveJournal and Blogger. This type of tool will be described in more detail later in this chapter.

One of the first genealogists to engage in regular blogging was Ralph Brandi. Beginning in February 2000 and continuing on a fairly regular basis through June 2004, Brandi's *Geneablogy* site (still online at www .brandi.org/geneablogy/) was one of the best examples of an early blog dedicated to describing the process of personal genealogical research. *Geneablogy* had all of the features of a basic blog:

- Content was organized into a series of *postings*, usually consisting of one or a few paragraphs of text, and sometimes accompanied by images or links to images.

- New content was automatically displayed at the top of the home page.

- Older content was displayed further down the home page.

- Each individual posting was automatically dated and time stamped, so that the reader would know exactly when it was posted.

- Each individual posting was provided with a unique URL, so that it could be linked to from anywhere else on the Web. (This unique URL is known as the posting's *permalink*, because it is a permanent link address that will never change, even if the posting is archived away from the home page as newer content is posted.)

- Once the home page reached a maximum number of postings, the oldest postings would be automatically archived by month, with links to each month's content from the home page.

- The text of the entire blog could be searched for a particular word, making it easier to locate a past posting.

Geneablogy

An occasional Journal about our experiences exploring our heritage

Friday, March 31, 2000

I sent away for some more vital records today. I sent for Grandpa Brandi's birth certificate, Great Grandpa Brandi's death certificate, and Great Grandpa Horbal's death certificate. Michigan charges $13 apiece for these, as opposed to Pennsylvania, which only charged $4. Ouch! Michigan does promise to act on requests within 1-5 days, though, which is a little quicker than Pennsylvania. We'll see; I don't suppose that genealogical requests take very high priority (and rightly so).

I'm hoping that between Grandpa's birth certificate and Great Grandpa Brandi's death certificate I can clear up the question of what Great Grandpa's middle name actually was. I'm hoping also that Grandpa's birth certificate will make crystal clear who his mother was and help dispel some of the confusion generated by Aunt Yola's and Aunt Zina's Social Security forms. And I hope, but don't expect, Great Grandpa Horbal's certificate will mention a little more clearly where in Poland he came from. I don't remember if Buscha died before or after him, but I think I remember that they went within less than a year of each other, so hopefully I'll get a better idea of which side of his death hers came on.

Posted at 3:28:59 PM link to this entry

I WANT TO
READ ABOUT

☐ Ralph's ancestors

☐ Brandi ❶
☐ Miller ❶
☐ Horbal ❶
☐ Zurbyk ❶

☐ Laura's ancestors

☐ Lombardo ❶
☐ Pantano ❶
☐ Saracco ❶

Ralph Brandi's *Geneablogy*, an early example of a blog dedicated to documenting personal genealogical research

Blogging and social networking

Although the blogging tools of the late 1990s provided a way for bloggers to create and maintain a blog as easily as they might create and send e-mail, the earliest blogs lacked some of the features needed to be considered social networking tools. Blogs were essentially one-way tools, with the bloggers putting their content out for others to read but not providing any easy way for the reader to provide feedback.

Certainly, some bloggers published their e-mail addresses on their blogs to make it possible for readers to reach them. In many cases, this e-mail address was included as part of an "About the Author" page that was linked to from the blog's home page, with a brief biography about the blogger, a photograph, and some reasons for the existence of the blog.

Even then, feedback did not automatically appear with the original posting. Eventually, blogging tools were refined and social networking features began to be added to blogs. These features now include:

- **Comments.** Readers have the ability to add a comment (usually at least a sentence but no more than a few paragraphs) to an individual blog posting. Postings that have comments are automatically marked with a message indicating how many comments have been left for that posting, and readers can read the comments of others. It is not unusual for a particularly interesting posting to result in dozens or hundreds of comments, with the original blogger taking part and a lot of interaction among the various commenters. Comments tend to breed more comments. In some cases, blog comments are moderated by the blogger so as to prevent abusive or off-topic comments. Blogs may also use a "CAPTCHA" feature (where the commenter has to read a distorted series of letters or words and type them into a box, proving that the commenter is a human being instead of a software program), in order to prevent *comment spam*.

- **Blogrolls.** A *blogroll* is a list of links to other blogs that are usually related in content to the original blog and are being recommended by the original blogger. Blogrolls make it easier for readers of blogs to discover new blogs of interest, and blogrolls also tend to create a "blogging community" among those bloggers who blog on the same topic. The blogroll is usually posted in a sidebar menu on the blog's home page.

- **Tags.** See Chapter 3 for a detailed description of tags. Blogging tools allow the blogger to add one or more tags to each posting. These tags create an automatic index to all blog postings, making it easier to find postings on the same subject within the blog. The index of tags may appear in a menu sidebar on the blog's home page.

- **RSS.** See Chapter 2 for a detailed description of RSS. Many blogs allow readers to "subscribe" to the blog so that they can be automatically notified when the blog contains new content. For some blogs, it is possible to subscribe separately to the blog postings and to the comments made about those postings.

Blogging and personal research

Although Ralph Brandi's *Geneablogy* has already been mentioned as a good example of a blog devoted to personal genealogical research, there is a more current example of this type of blog that also includes the social networking features of comments, a blogroll, tags, RSS for entries, and RSS for comments: *Steve's Genealogy Blog*, published by Stephen J. Danko and available online at stephendanko.com. This blog has been regularly maintained since April 2006. *Steve's Genealogy Blog* provides a detailed look at Danko's personal genealogical research, including his research methodology, displays of documents he has discovered, and his accompanying analysis and conclusions.

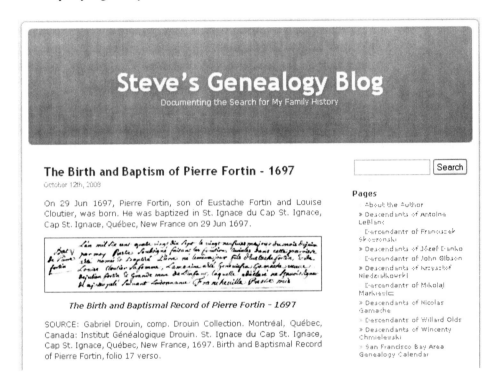

Stephen J. Danko's *Steve's Genealogy Blog*, a research blog with social networking features

Because Danko allows for comments on his postings, he has been rewarded with feedback on his analysis and many extra pairs of eyes to examine and interpret original documents. The quality of his analysis and presentation has resulted in his blog being linked to many other genealogy blogs and websites. Over time, the content of his blog has expanded from his specific personal research to more general content related to genealogy education and to news-type blogging from genealogy conferences.

Blogging, news, and personal opinion

While it is clear from the example of *Steve's Genealogy Blog* that blogging can be effectively used as a personal genealogy research tool, blogging has long been used as a way for organizations to publicize their activities, online journalists to broadcast the news, and anyone to offer their take on the issues of the day. These categories tend to blend into one another, but here are some specific examples in the genealogy world:

- Libraries, archives, and other repositories use blogs to highlight new acquisitions, alert visitors to temporary or permanent changes in hours, notify users of changes in policies and procedures, and publicize upcoming events.

- Genealogy societies use blogs to advertise upcoming meetings, increase awareness of local projects and events, and replace printed newsletters. National societies may even create specialized blogs just for news about upcoming national conferences.

- Genealogy-related companies use blogs to highlight new products and services and announce sales events. They may include educational articles to attract readership.

- Genealogy writers and speakers use blogs to highlight their writing and speaking activities and may include news, educational articles, and opinion pieces as part of the content.

- Genealogists, in general, use blogs to share news with the rest of the genealogy community and offer their opinions on issues relating to genealogy.

An example of a genealogy blog that serves as an online newsletter—offering a combination of news, opinion, and educational content—is *Eastman's Online Genealogy Newsletter (EOGN)*, published in blog format by Dick Eastman since June 1, 2004 and available online at blog.eogn.com. *EOGN* is commercially sponsored for its free content and is also available as a "Plus Edition," with additional content available only to paid subscribers. *EOGN* supports a number of social networking features, including comments, tags, and a blogroll.

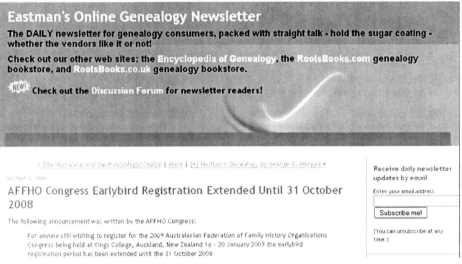

Eastman's Online Genealogy Newsletter (EOGN), a blog providing news, opinion, and educational content, published by Dick Eastman in blog format since June 1, 2004

Finding blogs of interest

While it would be possible to locate interesting genealogy-related blogs by beginning with the examples provided and then using blogrolls to move from one blog to another, there are more efficient ways to jump directly to blogs of potential interest.

Cyndi's List, available online at www.cyndislist.com, currently provides a list of over 70 popular genealogy blogs. This page is located at www.cyndislist.com/blogs.htm.

The *Genealogy Blog Finder*, maintained by Chris Dunham as a service of his blog, *The Genealogue*, is located at blogfinder.genealogue.com. This search engine currently searches the contents of over 1,100 genealogy-related blogs. You can search only the titles and descriptions of the blogs (in order to find a blog on a topic of interest) or the contents of the postings (in order to find a specific relevant posting).

Although blogs, like any other websites, can be individually bookmarked, it is usually more useful to subscribe to a blog using the blog's RSS feature so that you can be notified when new content has been added to the blog. In this way, it is possible to keep up with the content of dozens, if not hundreds, of blogs.

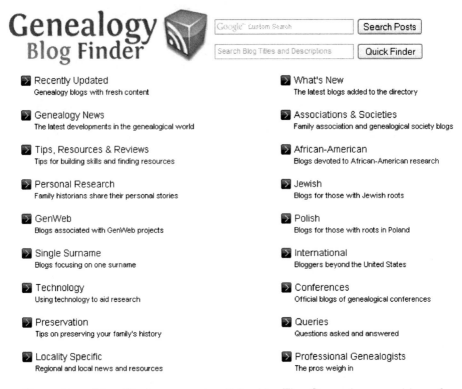

Genealogy Blog Finder, a service linked to *The Genealogue*, a blog of genealogy news and humor published by Chris Dunham

Creating and maintaining your own blog(s)

You can become part of the social networking aspects of the genealogy blogging community by reading and subscribing to blogs and then commenting on postings of interest. But to become a full member of the genealogy blogging community, you will want to create your own genealogy-related blog. You might do this on behalf of your local genealogy society, or you might choose instead to create a personal blog about genealogy news, offering up your opinions about genealogy topics or documenting your ongoing personal research.

Regardless of your reasons for blogging, you'll find it helpful to begin with an easy-to-use blog publishing system (editing tool and hosting service). Fortunately, there is one very popular blogging tool that requires no special software other than your existing web browser and that also provides free hosting for your blog. Since 2003, that publishing system has been part of the integrated online tools offered by Google. The tool is Blogger (online at blogger.com).

Blogger is a free blog publishing system provided by Google

Because Blogger is part of Google's suite of online tools, it uses the same free Google Account that you may already be using for iGoogle, Gmail, Google Calendar, Google Docs, Picasa Web Albums, Google Reader, YouTube, and Google Groups. If you haven't already created a Google Account, you can create your account when you first visit the Blogger site.

Associated with your Blogger account is a User Profile (a standard feature of social networking). The Blogger User Profile, which can be kept private or shared with anyone who views your blog(s), can include your real name, your e-mail address, your photo, an audio clip (such as a welcoming voice message from you), your gender, your birth date (with or without year), various URLs related to you, an account where you receive Instant Messages (IMs), your city/state/country, your occupation, and additional information about your interests and favorite choices in movies, music, and books. As a genealogist, you might use your User Profile as a way to identify for others your research surnames, geographic areas, and ethnic groups of interest.

When you log in to Blogger, you are shown your "Dashboard," a page that lists all of your blogs, with a link that allows you to create a new one. For each of your existing blogs, you are shown how many postings it contains, when it was last updated, and how many comments have been posted that need to be moderated. For each blog, you can also add a new posting, edit previous postings, change the settings for that blog, change the blog's template (see below), or see what the current blog looks like.

Blogger's Dashboard, used to edit the User Profile and manage multiple blogs

A *template* is a particular blog design (layout, font, colors, etc.). Blogger provides a large number of templates from which to choose, and you can change your blog's template later without affecting its content. You can also customize templates if you are comfortable using the XHTML language to design web pages.

Once you have created your blog and customized its layout and settings to your liking, you are ready to make your first posting. Creating a blog posting is very similar to creating a piece of e-mail, and publishing your posting is very similar to sending e-mail. For instance, a typical blog posting consists of a title (like an e-mail's subject line), followed by content.

Blogger's Posting screen, used to create and publish your blog's content

As with many e-mail programs, you can use Blogger's word-processing-style features to edit your content, including fonts, paragraph alignment, hyperlinks, bullets and numbering, spell checking, the addition of images, and so forth. You can save postings to publish later, and you can edit postings that have been previously published (such as when you discover an error or typo). You can also delete postings.

Notice that you can label a posting with any number of labels. This is Blogger's implementation of tags, and for a genealogist, this could be used for surnames, place names, types of records discussed, etc. Because you can add images to a posting, this is where you might include digitized images of genealogical source documents or photos of family and ancestors.

Getting involved with blogging

To get involved with blogging as part of social networking, you might take the following incremental steps:

1. **Find and read** one or more genealogy blogs of interest using the *Genealogy Blog Finder*.

2. **Subscribe** to one or more blogs using a feed aggregator (see Chapter 2 for how to do this).

3. **Comment** on a blog posting that you have enjoyed, disagree with, or can provide an answer to.

4. **Create** your own blog about genealogy using Blogger.

5. **Tag** your blog postings so that others can find them more easily.

6. **Maintain** a blogroll on your blog to help others find interesting blogs that you enjoy.

7. **Allow others to comment** about your blog postings.

Chapter 6:
Wikis

How groups create a network of information

wiki (noun): A website that provides an easy way for multiple individuals to create and edit the pages of the site without having to know any specialized formatting language

Introduction

In the earlier days of the Web, at least two hurdles limited the creation and regular maintenance of websites: Creating and editing web pages required a basic knowledge of HTML, and website security often limited access to a single individual, the "webmaster." Without a large (and therefore expensive) professional staff, the idea of creating a reasonably current encyclopedia online would have seemed ludicrous. Then, in 1994, Ward Cunningham created a way for multiple individuals to gain access to a website for page creation and editing without having to know any HTML. This "quick" way to create and maintain a website was given the name "wiki" (a Hawaiian word associated with the fast shuttle buses of the Honolulu International Airport). And this wiki concept eventually led to an online encyclopedia that didn't require a large, expensive professional staff.

Despite the value of this tool among many different kinds of user communities, it is possible that most Internet users would be unaware of the wiki concept if it were not for Wikipedia, the online encyclopedia that features over two million entries in its English-language version. It is tempting to go to one extreme or another in rendering an opinion about Wikipedia. Some may regard it as the greatest advancement in information research since Google. Others may condemn it as a hodgepodge of unreliable content contributed by anonymous users. A more supportable opinion, unsurprisingly, is somewhere in the middle. As with the Web itself, Wikipedia is an amazing assemblage of information, much of it accurate and highly useful, but any user of Wikipedia should use critical thinking skills to evaluate its content.

For a genealogist, Wikipedia can be a valuable reference source, providing basic information on the history, geography, language, culture, and technology that we may run across as we research our families. However, as with any other general-purpose encyclopedia, Wikipedia is not likely to have pages dedicated to explaining unusual genealogical terms or to providing basic guidance in doing research within specific ethnic groups. Fortunately, there is a wiki dedicated to exactly that purpose: Dick Eastman's *Encyclopedia of Genealogy*.

Encyclopedia of Genealogy (eogen)—overview

In late 2004, Dick Eastman, perhaps best known for *Eastman's Online Genealogy Newsletter*, made a wiki available to the genealogical community that would serve as a type of "encyclopedia." The wiki, entitled *Encyclopedia of Genealogy* (abbreviated as *eogen* and available online at eogen.com), was designed to serve as a general online reference source for genealogists, with a variety of genealogy-related content not found elsewhere in a single location. Its index currently consists of approximately 900 entries, including non-English terms for family relationships; genealogical repositories and organizations; legal and medical terms; and terms specific to genealogical methodology. Here is the top of its home page:

Notice that the entire *eogen* can be searched by using the box at the top right of the screen. Another useful option is to use the Index feature to browse an alphabetical list of articles:

Index

A | B | C | D | E | F | G | H | I | J | K | L | M | N | O | P | Q | R | S | T | U |
V | W | X | Y | Z | É |

A

A2 A

AAGRA

AASP

Abiatico

Abp

Abstract

abt

Abuela

Abuelo

Acadian "Dit" Names

Individual entries are generally written in an encyclopedia style and may contain links to other items in the *eogen* or to external websites. Here is the beginning of the entry for "Ahnentafel":

Ahnentafel

An Ahnentafel is a list of one's ancestors with each one numbered in a sequential manner that makes it easy to calculate relationships. The Ahnentafel method is the most common method of numbering ancestors

Ahnentafel is a German word that translates as "ancestor table" or, literally, a list of one's ancestors. The same numbering system is sometimes called the Sosa-Stradonitz System, named after the Spanish genealogist Hieronymus/Jerome de Sosa, who first used it in 1676, and after the German genealogist Stephan Kekulé von Stradonitz [1863-1933], who popularized it in his 1896 Ahnentafel Atlas.

Encyclopedia of Genealogy (eogen)—editing the content

As with most wikis, the pages of *eogen* are intended to be created and maintained by a large number of volunteers, but at the same time, safeguards are in place to avoid abuse of the system by anonymous users. In order to contribute to *eogen*, users must first go through a free, one-time registration process, and then log in to the system:

Login

User Name:

Password:

Remember Me: ☐

Login

Register

Forgot your user name or password?

Need Help?

Once you are logged in, each page of *eogen* will automatically include an "Edit this page" button:

TRAILS   Edit this page

TRAILS is an online database available through the Hillsborough County Public Library Cooperative. Its primary use for genealogists is that it contains an index to obituaries published in the Tampa Tribune and its predecessors from 1895 to about 1987. It also contains entries for newspaper and magazine articles dealing with Tampa Bay and Florida history. Each entry contains date and page references which can then be used to locate the original article or obituary on microfilm. Detailed information can be found at the following link:

http://www.hcplc.org/hcplc/ig/userguides/uthor/thortrails.html

Clicking the "Edit this page" button brings up a screen that resembles a screen for composing e-mail or a word processing document:

What looks like an e-mail's subject line is the word or term being described. The bulk of the editing screen is taken up by the box to enter the text and the formatting options above the box. Those who know HTML can use the "Code Editor" or "Text Editor" options to directly enter the HTML formatting codes.

In this particular wiki, registered users have the option of being notified of all changes to any of the entries or only to those that are not marked as "Minor Edits." Those who are editing entries can use the "Minor Edit" checkbox in cases where they are making only small corrections to grammar, spelling, or punctuation, instead of significantly changing the meaning of existing content or adding new content.

The distorted graphic of a word (known as a "CAPTCHA") is intended to ensure that a human being is manually attempting to edit the wiki instead of an automated system attempting to spam the wiki with inappropriate content.

Once the editing has been completed, the user can save the results, which become instantly visible to all those who use the wiki after that point.

Encyclopedia of Genealogy (eogen)—version history

The other tabs on the editing screen lead to ways to provide additional information about the content of the entry, place the entry within a navigational tree structure, and view the history of the entry. The most interesting and useful of these (and one of the primary features that sets a wiki apart from other kinds of websites) is the display of the entry's history:

Version History for TRAILS | Close Editor |

Click a version number below to view it. To replace the current version with a previous version, edit the version you want to revert to and save. A new version will be created. Click Diff to see what changed between versions.

Version			Date	Title	User	Description
4	Edit	Diff	5:54 PM	TRAILS	drewsmith	Newspaper title was italicized
3	Edit	Diff	Jul 16, 2006	TRAILS	JohnCardinal	Revoved FONT tag so link looks like link
2	Edit	Diff	Jul 13, 2006	TRAILS	reastman	Converted URL to a "clickable" link
1	Edit	Diff	Jul 13, 2006	TRAILS	SALMONFORGEY	

Let's face it: When you have a collaborative project of this nature, you want some accountability of exactly who did what and when, in order to help iron out misunderstandings and minimize abuse. Even if all of the wiki's contributors are well intentioned, mistakes will be made. Fortunately, most wikis are designed to save every past version of each entry, so mistakes can be un-done without too much trouble.

PBwiki—creating your own wiki

Wikis do not have to be general purpose encyclopedias (like Wikipedia) or even encyclopedias limited to covering a particular discipline (such as genealogical research). A wiki could serve any purpose where there would be an advantage in having a website hosting linked content with the option of having many potential contributors. A genealogical researcher could create a wiki as a way to record and preserve family or local history, with each page representing an individual ancestor, ancestral family, or ancestral place. If in the past you have considered the idea of having a website about your ancestors but dismissed the idea because you lacked knowledge of HTML, or you didn't have time to do it by yourself but didn't know a way to have a collaborative website, having your own wiki may be the solution. Fortunately, just as is true with blogs, a number of online services provide free tools to maintain and host a wiki. For the remainder of this chapter, we'll use PBwiki (available online at pbwiki.com) as our example of such an online service.

In 2005, the PBwiki online service was founded with the idea that creating and maintaining a wiki should be as easy as making a peanut butter sandwich (hence the name). While PBwiki sells its services to businesses (for more than three collaborators), it also provides free wiki services to businesses (three or fewer collaborators), educational users, and personal users (individuals, clubs, and groups). Free usage for personal users includes a wiki of up to two gigabytes of storage, a limited choice of color schemes, an unlimited number of individual pages, one RSS-format web feed for the entire wiki, and the ability of the wiki owner to allow for collaborators and specify what the collaborators are allowed to do. Free accounts can be upgraded to varying levels of paid accounts so as to add such features as more storage, an individual RSS-format web feed for each wiki page, and more control over the appearance of the wiki. (If you need to understand how RSS works, see Chapter 2.)

Once you have created your free PBwiki account, you can create your own wiki. In this example, I'm going to create a wiki for my research into the Boddie family:

Create your wiki

| Choose a wiki name | http:// | boddiefamily | .pbwiki.com |

What is this wiki for? ◉ For individuals
Personal use, groups, clubs

○ For education
Classrooms, libraries, schools, universities

○ For business
Teams, workgroups, enterprise

Use PBwiki 2.0

☑ Yes, please make this a PBwiki 2.0 wiki
Learn more about PBwiki 2.0

Create my wiki

Notice that the wiki name you choose will determine the URL that your wiki will use. After you name your wiki and click on the "Create my wiki" button, you will have the option of setting the basic wiki privacy options (and the unsurprising request to explicitly agree to the online service's terms of service):

Welcome to
boddiefamily.pbwiki.com

Choose your wiki's security settings
You can change these later by going to wiki settings.

Who can view this wiki?
◉ Anyone
○ Only people I invite or approve

Who can edit this wiki?
○ Anyone with an account
◉ Only people I invite or approve

Accept PBwiki Terms of Service
☑ I agree to the PBwiki terms of service.

[Take me to my wiki]

Having already seen the examples of Wikipedia and the *Encyclopedia of Genealogy*, it may not have occurred to you that a wiki could be set up so that it could not be viewed by the general public. But for a genealogical researcher, this feature allows for a wiki that may contain personal details about the living, viewable only by those individuals given permission by the wiki owner. The downside to making the wiki private, of course, is that it makes it more difficult for your wiki's contents to be discovered by distant relatives and other genealogical researchers.

Notice also that you're not given the opportunity to allow anonymous contributions to your wiki. You can open up the wiki for editing to anyone who has a PBwiki account or limit contributions to specific individuals whom you have approved. Regardless, this provides some accountability and limits abuse.

Click the "Take me to my wiki" button, and you're done. All you have left to do is create content and invite others to view (if private) or edit your wiki.

PBwiki—a few special features

I won't bother to repeat the concepts that were already covered in the discussion of *eogen*, such as creating and editing wiki pages or viewing a page's history. Instead, I'll focus on a few features not already covered or those available only to wiki owners.

You can add one or more tags to each page, which can make it easier to find a relevant page when searching the wiki. (If you are unfamiliar with tags, see Chapter 3.) This is as simple as clicking on the "Add tags" menu choice on the right while you are viewing the wiki page. For a genealogist, appropriate tags might be such things as surnames, place names, or record types:

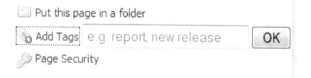

If you are editing the page instead of just viewing it, you will also have a box below the content area to add a list of tags.

The wiki owner has a large number of options over the appearance of the wiki and the privacy settings for the entire wiki or for individual pages. Most critical may be the ability to add readers (to a private wiki) or collaborators. This PBwiki screen will give you an idea of what's possible:

Manage Users

Add a user

Email address   Add Multiple Emails

Permission level   Writer   ▾   [**Add user**]
                   Learn more about permission levels

All Users (1)

▾ USER   PERMISSION LEVEL

🔒 Drew Smith   Administrator   ▾
   drewsmithtpa@gmail.com

When you invite others to read your wiki (if private instead of public) or collaborate with you on editing your wiki, you can set their assigned "role." For a private wiki, you can limit someone to being a "Reader." For any kind of wiki, you can allow them to be a "Writer" (adding new content or editing existing content), an "Editor" (renaming and deleting pages), or an "Administrator" (changing wiki settings and inviting new collaborators).

Final comments about wikis

While other kinds of online services may be designed specifically for genealogists so that you can collaborate with others about the names, dates, and locations of your shared research, a wiki can make it easier for you to share and preserve an ever-changing online family history and attract unknown researchers to your site.

Getting involved with wikis

To get involved with wikis as part of your genealogical research, you might take the following incremental steps:

1. **Visit** the *Encyclopedia of Genealogy* and search for a topic of interest.

2. **Register** for an account on the *Encyclopedia of Genealogy* and edit an existing page or create a new one for a topic not yet covered.

3. **Create** your own wiki by setting up a free account with PBwiki.

4. **Allow** others to contribute to your wiki.

Chapter 7:
Collaborative editing

How groups co-edit a document

Introduction

If you were to look at lists of printed family histories, you would quickly notice that the vast majority are written by a single author. Even with multiple authors, it may simply be the case that one author began the work and another author added to the work at a later date. Or different authors wrote different chapters. Things didn't change much when family histories were created using a word processor instead of a typewriter. When a manuscript for a family history had to "live" on a single computer, it was difficult for multiple authors to collaborate on the same text at the same time. It should not be surprising that so many family histories still have a single author identified with the work (although additional contributors may be acknowledged).

In the age of the Internet, it became feasible for co-authors to e-mail the draft of a manuscript back and forth, but even this was relatively cumbersome. To facilitate collaboration on a family history document, there would need to be a way for the collaborators to share a common view of the current document and make edits essentially simultaneously. This means that the document would need to be online someplace where all of the collaborators (but nobody else) would have access. A number of online services have come into existence in order to offer the ability to collaborate on documents. The best known of these is Google Docs.

Google Docs—getting started

If you already have a Google Account (such as one for Gmail or to use a personalized iGoogle screen), then you automatically have access to

Google Docs. If you don't have one yet, you can quickly create a free Google Account by going to the main Google page (www.google.com), clicking on the "Sign in" link at the top right corner of the screen, and then clicking the "Create an account now" link.

Once you have signed into your Google Account, you can get directly to Google Docs by visiting docs.google.com:

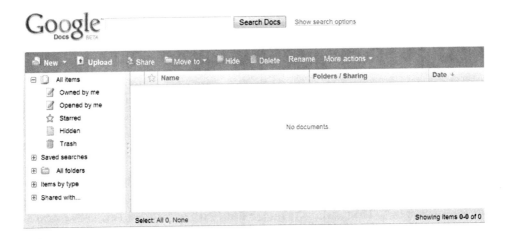

When you first begin to use Google Docs, you will be presented with a list of all the documents you own, as well as any document owned by others who may have given you access. (Google Docs allows you to edit and collaborate on documents, spreadsheets, and presentations, but for the purpose of this chapter, I'll be limiting my example to editing and collaborating on a document, such as the manuscript of a family history.)

If you have already begun a document on your home computer using a standard word processor, you can upload that document into Google Docs:

Upload a File

Browse your computer to select a file to upload:

Browse...

Or enter the URL of a file on the web:

What do you want to call it? (if different than the file name)

Upload File

Types of files that you can upload:

Documents (up to 500KB)
- HTML files and plain text (.txt).
- Microsoft Word (.doc), Rich Text (.rtf), OpenDocument Text (.odt) and StarOffice (.sxw).

Presentations (up to 10MB from your computer, 2MB from the web, 500KB via email)
- Microsoft PowerPoint (.ppt, .pps).

At the time of this writing, Google Docs cannot yet import files in .docx format (the latest Microsoft Word format). You would need to save a .docx document into one of the formats supported by Google Docs before uploading it.

Or, you could begin a brand-new document in Google Docs, just as you would in a word processing program on your home computer:

As the screen shot suggests, Google Docs provides a large number of the standard features associated with standard word processing programs, including fonts, footnotes, headers, footers, tables of contents, a spelling checker, tables, and the ability to insert links and graphics. Unfortunately, Google Docs does not yet provide one feature necessary to producing a good family history: the ability to automatically generate an index to the manuscript. You can always, however, download the finished document to a computer that has a word processor capable of generating an index.

Because the document is saved online, you have access to it from any computer connected to the Internet. You don't have to worry about losing it as the result of a computer theft or hard drive crash.

A few limits to be aware of: Each document may be no larger than 500K, so a large family history manuscript might have to be broken into individual chapters. Each embedded image can be up to 2MB. And you can have as many as 5,000 different documents and 5,000 images.

Google Docs—collaborating

Even if you never intended to collaborate with anyone else on your family history manuscript, you would still find much to like about Google Docs. You could e-mail a copy of the manuscript to anyone as an attachment or have Google Docs create a web version of your manuscript that could be posted on a website. But the social networking feature of Google Docs is that you can make your document private—allowing only a select list of individuals to view it—and, whether private or not, allow only a select list of individuals to edit the document with you. By clicking on the "Share" button and choosing "Share with others," you can manage who can view and who can edit the document:

Invite people

⦿ as collaborators   ○ as viewers

```

```

Separate email addresses with commas.
Choose from contacts

> Invite collaborators

Advanced permissions

☑ Collaborators may invite others
  Only the owner may change this

☑ Invitations may be used by anyone
  Allows mailing lists Learn more

This document is not shared.
Preview document as a viewer
View RSS feed of document changes

Collaborators (0)
Collaborators may edit the document and invite more people.

Viewers (0)
Viewers may see the document but not edit it.

Notice that you can choose to let your new collaborators recruit additional collaborators, perhaps as a way to further the workload of creating and editing the document. You are limited to a maximum of 200 viewers/collaborators, and only 10 people may view/edit the document at the same time.

If you already have your contacts managed by Google (such as for Gmail), you can access your list of contacts for the purpose of inviting viewers and collaborators.

One last useful feature of Google Docs: Anyone with the ability to view or edit the document can subscribe to an RSS-format web feed for the document, so that they will be automatically notified of changes to the document. (See Chapter 2 for more information on how RSS works.)

Getting involved with collaborative editing

To get involved with collaborative editing as part of your genealogical research, you might take the following incremental steps:

1. **Create** a Google Account (if you don't already have one).

2. **Create** a document, such as a draft of a family history, using Google Docs.

3. **Invite** others to view or edit your document.

Chapter 8:
Photo and video sharing

Letting the world see your photo albums and home movies

Introduction

Images move us in ways that text cannot. (Of course, the reverse is also true.) I have fond childhood memories of looking through old photo albums with members of my family, or watching the latest home movie created by a favorite uncle visiting during a holiday. Although I have no idea what may have happened to my late uncle's old film reels from decades ago, I still possess copies of many of my family's cherished pictures, even though nearly all of the individuals pictured are long gone.

The digital world has not only made the creation of photos and videos far easier than in previous generations but, when combined with the Web, has also made it practical to share those digital images with anyone in the world, known or unknown. The photo you possess of a great-grandmother, published by you on the Web, may be discovered and enjoyed by a distant relative. The video you create of a trip to your ancestral town may bring family history to life for your scattered cousins.

Flickr—an overview

While there are a large number of different websites for hosting and sharing photographs, the largest and likely best known is Flickr (online at flickr.com), a service of Yahoo! With over 3 billion photos in its database, Flickr's free service allows individuals to upload 100 megabytes of new photos per month and display their 200 most recent photos. Paid accounts (approximately $25 per year) have no limits. It should be noted that Flickr can also be used for sharing videos, but we'll be addressing only its photo sharing service in this chapter. When you first visit Flickr, you'll see a sample photo:

You can search Flickr's huge database of photos by using the search box on the home page. For instance, if I search for "genealogy," I get approximately 40,000 hits. Here is the top part of the results screen:

Search   Photos   Groups   People

genealogy   SEARCH   Advanced Search
                                                            Search by Camera
◉ Full text   ○ Tags only

✓ We found **39,968 results** matching genealogy.

View: Most relevant • Most recent • Most interesting   Show: Details • Thumbnails

Genealogy / Family Tree Visualization
by Walter Rafelsberger

3 comments   ⭐ 10 faves

Tagged with family,motion,tree,film...
Uploaded January 15, 2007

See more of Walter Rafelsberger's photos, or visit his profile.

Notice that from this screen you gain access to a more powerful search interface. You can search the "full text," meaning the photo titles, the name of the photos' publisher, the descriptions of the photos, and the associated tags, or you can limit your search to just the tags. (If you are unfamiliar with tags, see Chapter 3.)

If you click on the "Advanced Search" link, you are rewarded with additional search options and tips on how to use them. Here are two of the most useful:

Search for

Tip: Use these options to look for an exact phrase or to exclude words or tags from your search. For example, search for photos tagged with "apple" but not "pie"

All of these words ▾	genealogy
All of these words	● Full text ○ Tags only
The exact phrase	
Any of these words	

None of these words:

Search by date

Tip: Use one or both dates to search for photos taken or posted within a certain time

	after	before
Photos taken ▾		
Photos taken	mm/dd/yyyy	mm/dd/yyyy
Posted		

The results of any search will display a list of photos that match your search parameters. You will get to see a clickable thumbnail (relatively smaller version) of each photo, the title of the photo, the name of the person who published the photo, the number of comments that have been added to the photo, the number of people who have marked the photo as a favorite, a list of tags associated with the photo, the dates on which the photo was taken and was uploaded to Flickr, a link to a collection of more photos by the same person, and a link to the person's profile.

Clicking on the photo's thumbnail will take you to the Flickr page for that photo, where you will gain access to a larger number of options and more information about the photo, including any comments that have been made about it. Not only will you be able to see a version of the photo larger than the previous thumbnail, but you may also be given the option to see even larger versions. Notice that the Flickr page for the photo has a unique, fixed URL, so you can bookmark the page for later use or use the URL for other kinds of sharing.

Flickr—tagging, commenting, and uploading

Searching for and viewing the photos of others is interesting, but the social networking aspects enter in when you respond to the photos of others (or when they respond to yours). But you will not be able to participate in these activities anonymously. Instead, you will need to create a free Flickr account tied to your e-mail address. As Flickr is one of the Yahoo! properties, you can use your existing Yahoo! ID (if you already have one). Otherwise, you can just go ahead and create a new Flickr account.

In Flickr, you can set up photos so that others can tag them and comment on them. (If the photo is not set up with those permissions, you won't see the options to tag or comment.) For example, you may find a photo uploaded by someone else where they forgot to tag the photo with the name of a person in the photo, the city in which the photo was taken, or a prominent object appearing in the photo. The photo's publisher will be notified of any added tags and will have final say in whether they remain with the photo or not.

Commenting on the photo (if allowed) provides a number of ways to respond to the photo's publisher. It's common for a commenter to give positive feedback on the photo. Others may use comments to ask for permission to use the photo in other venues or make the photo's publisher aware of other individuals and groups who may share the publisher's interest in the photo. Because the photo's publisher is notified of new comments and can comment on his or her own photos, the list of comments for a photo may turn into a dialogue between the publisher and other interested individuals. For a genealogist who has posted a photo of a tombstone or ancestral building, this dialogue can be quite valuable!

Uploading your own photos to Flickr is an easy process, and Flickr takes you through it step-by-step:

Upload photos to Flickr

You've used **0%** of your 100 MB limit this month - that leaves **100 MB**. Upgrade?

Step 1:

Choose photos

Did you hear? With a pro account, you can upload video to Flickr now! Learn more about vi

Step 2:

Upload photos

Step 3:

Notice that you'll be reminded of your monthly upload limitation (after all, they'd like you to switch from the free version to a paid version with no limitations). Clicking on the "Choose photos" link will take you to a standard window on your own computer system to locate the photos. After you have selected the photo to be uploaded, Flickr will give you some options:

File	Size	Remove?
IMGP0516.JPG	2.18 MB	🗑

1 file Add More	**Total: 2.18 MB**	

Set privacy / Show more upload settings

- ○ Private (only you see them)
  - ☐ Visible to Friends
  - ☐ Visible to Family
- ◉ Public (anyone can see them)

Upload Photos

While the default privacy setting is "Public" (so that anyone can search Flickr to find and see your photo), the available privacy options should make you feel better about sharing pictures of living family members (especially of children), to prevent them from being viewed by strangers. Under the "Show more upload settings" are additional privacy settings, such as keeping a public photo from appearing in search results (in other words, only those who know the direct URL can see it).

After you have uploaded your photo, you will be given the option to add a brief title (otherwise, it just uses the file name), any number of tags, and a longer textual description. Don't worry about perfection at this point (or if you're in a hurry and want to skip this step for now), since you can always go back later and edit the title, tags, and description. Here's what your finished uploaded photo might look like:

George and Lizzie Martin family of Newberry, SC

Add your comment

A few last comments before we leave Flickr: You can keep in touch with other Flickr users (and quickly jump to their photos) by establishing them as "contacts." You can organize your photos by "sets." As a result, entire family networks of genealogical researchers can share their ancestral photos and make them available to the public to attract other researchers.

YouTube—an overview

While Flickr's "reputation" may be nothing more scandalous than a place to upload family vacation photos and maybe a few silly images from teenage spring-break parties, YouTube (online at youtube.com) may appear in the minds of many as a place catering primarily to rock music videos and strange "watch me do this" recordings that are hopeful candidates for TV blooper shows. But YouTube has been ranked as one of the most visited websites on the entire Web (behind only Google and Yahoo!), and it's not just because of music videos and recorded silliness.

YouTube's tens of millions of videos (most of which fail to exceed ten minutes long) include a significant number of instructional videos, and some of those are even about genealogy! You may find interviews with well-known genealogists, video versions of family stories, and travelogues of ancestral towns. Searching for videos in YouTube is as easy as searching for photos in Flickr:

The results page will show you a list of links to videos, sorted by relevance to your search. Parts of the results screen are shown next:

If you prefer, you can re-sort the results list by the date on which each video was uploaded, how many times it has been viewed, or how highly it has been rated. If you visit YouTube regularly (or only want fresh content), you can limit your search to videos uploaded in the past day, past week, or past month. Notice that each video's screenshot gives you the length of the video in minutes and seconds, and the beginning of the video's description and the ID of the video's uploader appears on the right.

Clicking on the video's screenshot or on its title will take you to the video's own page (which has a unique URL you can bookmark), but be fore-warned: As soon as the page appears, the video will start to play. If you are fast, you can click on the pause button at the bottom left of the video. Other-wise, you may need to remember to reduce the volume on your computer's speakers so as not to accidentally disturb others in your household!

Displayed below the video are comments by other viewers (similar to those seen on Flickr), and a list of videos of a similar nature (usually on the same subject) appears in a scrollable window on the right.

YouTube—getting more involved

If you want to engage in social networking with users of YouTube, you'll need to create a free account. Fortunately, YouTube is a subsidiary of Google, so you won't have to go to the trouble of creating a free You-Tube account if you already have a Google Account. Once you sign in with your YouTube account and navigate to a particular video, you'll see a com-ment box where you can post your own comment about the video, up to 500 characters long.

But the fun truly begins when you decide to share your own videos with the rest of the world. You may have digitized some older home mov-ies, recorded a recent family event or reunion, or created a slide presenta-tion about one of your ancestors with your own voiceover and background music. Regardless of the type of video you want to share, the process is the same. First, you'd click on the Upload button found on the top right of the YouTube screen and choose "Video File":

Upload ▼
　　Video File
Quick Capture

If you're worried about issues such as your video's length, its format, or other technical issues, don't worry, as the next screen will address these:

Video File Upload

Select a video to upload.

Browse...

Upload Video

About Uploading

- Upload up to 10 videos at a time
- Best video formats for YouTube
- Up to 1 GB in size.

It should be noted that YouTube will not be happy with you if you upload video content that is copyrighted by others (if they have not given you permission).

If some of the terminology being used is new to you, don't worry. While creating and editing video content is certainly more complicated than working only with still photos, YouTube provides a free online handbook to get you started and offer you tips on getting the best results.

RootsTube—genealogy videos made by everyone

Although YouTube reaches an enormous audience, you may feel that you'd like to target other genealogists with your videos. If so, you may find it useful to submit your YouTube video to Roots Television (online at rootstelevision.com), a site that showcases original genealogical programming. Roots Television has set aside one of its "channels" (collections of related videos) for user-contributed videos, a channel it calls "RootsTube." To see the RootsTube submission form, which includes information about video file formats and size limitations, visit the following URL:

www.rootstelevision.com/submit_rootstube.php

Getting involved with photo and video sharing

To get involved with photo and video sharing as part of your genealogical research, you might take the following incremental steps:

1. **Search** Flickr for photos of interest or YouTube for videos
   of interest.

2. **Subscribe** to an RSS-format web feed from Flickr or
   YouTube.

3. **Create** a Flickr account and comment on or tag a photo.

4. **Create** a YouTube account and comment on a video.

5. **Create** a digital photo using a digital camera or by scanning
   a printed photo, or create a digital video using a camcorder.

6. **Upload** your photo to Flickr or your video to YouTube.

7. **Contribute** your YouTube video to RootsTube.

Chapter 9:
Social bookmarking

Discovering sites recommended by others

Introduction

When you first started using the World Wide Web, you may rapidly have become weary of typing and then re-typing a highly useful URL, or become annoyed with yourself that you had forgotten the URL to a favorite site. Then you discovered that your browser had a feature known as "bookmarks" or "favorites," a way to save for future reference the URL of the site you were currently viewing. This meant never again having to re-type a long, complex URL or worrying that you'd forget the URL for a site that you might not use again for a year or more.

Today, it is hard to imagine using browsers without bookmarks. Even so, you feel the pain of being without your handy list of bookmarks when you are using a computer other than your usual home or work computer (and if you regularly use more than one computer, Murphy's Law dictates that the bookmark you need is saved on the other system). It can also be cumbersome to share useful bookmarks with friends and colleagues, since that usually involves some copying and pasting.

There are solutions to these problems. Let's enter the world of social bookmarking.

Delicious—an overview

One of the oldest and best known online services for sharing bookmarks is Delicious (known prior to August 2008 as del.icio.us), available online at delicious.com. Delicious, a free service owned by Yahoo!, provides the following features:

- a very large searchable database of bookmarks shared by Delicious account holders
- the ability to create and store a private set of bookmarks that can be accessed from any computer
- the ability to share bookmarks with others
- the ability to describe and tag bookmarks (whether private or shared)

Let's start at the Delicious home page:

A good place to start is the search box, in order to look for bookmarks of interest. Let's see how many bookmarks can be found using the search term of "genealogy":

We get nearly 62,000 hits:

See all bookmarks tagged (genealogy)   Search all of Delicious for "genealogy" →

🔍 **Everybody's bookmarks**   61955 results - show all →

Geni - **Genealogy** - Free Family Tree SAVE   3192

First saved by: arachno1999   family   familytree   web2.0   social   (genealogy)

MyHeritage - Family 2.0 and **Genealogy** SAVE   2947

First saved by: Michelr   recognition   photo   fun   web2.0   (genealogy)

FamilySearch.org - Family History and **Genealogy** Records SAVE   1897

First saved by: holgi   family   history   search   reference   (genealogy)

Cyndi's List of **Genealogy** Sites on the Internet SAVE   1266

First saved by: cdauvil   reference   research   history   search   (genealogy)

Genealogy, Family Trees and Family History Records online - Ancestry.com SAVE   1767

First saved by: santi   family   ancestry   history   reference   (genealogy)

For each bookmark, you get to see the title of the webpage, the ID of the first Delicious user who bookmarked it, a list of tags associated with the bookmark (which helps to further describe it), and the number of Delicious users who have bookmarked it (a measure of the website's popularity).

Because a webpage may be about genealogy without having the word "genealogy" in its title, our previous search may have missed a lot of bookmarked sites about genealogy. By clicking on one of the gray "genealogy" tags, you can do another kind of search that looks for every bookmark that has been tagged by some Delicious user as being related to genealogy. This gives us over 100,000 hits. Of course, you could narrow your search by including an additional search term, such as a surname, the name of an ethnic group, or a place name. If someone has bookmarked a site for Smith genealogy or Polish genealogy, a combined search will locate it.

Delicious—creating your own bookmarks and sharing them

Although Delicious is designed to make it easy to share bookmarks with others, you can certainly use it to maintain a private list of bookmarks that you can access from any computer you are using. When you create a free Delicious account, Delicious asks if you want to install an extra button into your browser. The button will make it easier to add a new-found website to your collection of bookmarks on Delicious. However, you can skip the step of adding the button and come back to it later if you change your mind. You'll find the "Tools" page within the Help area:

Tools

Bookmarking buttons and add-ons for your browser or website

Browser buttons for saving bookmarks

Firefox Bookmarks add-on – tag buttons and optional integration of your bookmarks

Internet Explorer buttons – tag buttons and optional integration of your bookmarks

Bookmarklet buttons for any browser – simple "Bookmark on Delicious" buttons

If you already have a large number of bookmarks on one or more personal computers, you can upload your existing bookmarks into Delicious. Delicious can usually detect what brand of browser you are using, so you'll be given instructions on how to do the import with your specific browser. The import procedure usually involves exporting your browser's bookmarks into a separate file on your computer, and then uploading that file to Delicious. The file must be no larger than 5MB.

Delicious gives you a number of options when you upload a file of bookmarks, including:

- whether or not to automatically add a tag to each imported bookmark (the default tag is "imported")

- whether or not to mark your imported bookmarks as private (the default is private)

- what option to take if your imported bookmark matches a bookmark that you have already created in Delicious (the default is to replace the Delicious bookmark with the imported one)

After you have decided on your import options, you can have Delicious notify you by e-mail when the upload has been completed.

Whether or not you import any bookmarks into Delicious, you can add bookmarks one at a time to Delicious whenever you discover a valuable website. If you are not using an installed Delicious button on your browser to do this, you can go to a Delicious screen to manually type in the URL. Let's go through the process with an example:

Save a new bookmark
Start by entering a URL

Did you know? Saving bookmarks to Delicious is much easier with our bookmarking tools

URL genealogyguys.com|

Next

Delicious automatically adds the title for the webpage (if it is already known to Delicious) and provides you with a screen to edit the URL, title, webpage description, and tags:

Save a new bookmark
Now add tags and notes

URL http://genealogyguys.com/

required

TITLE The Genealogy Guys Podcast

required

NOTES

1000 characters left

TAGS

space separated, 128 characters per tag

Do Not Share

Save   Cancel

Tags   People

Sort Alpha | Frequency

▼ Popular

genealogy podcast blog blogs podcasts history learning

Notice that you can mark the bookmark as private by checking the "Do Not Share" checkbox below the "TAGS" box. Once you save the bookmark, Delicious returns you to your list of bookmarks:

Now you immediately know how many other Delicious users have the same bookmark. If you have not marked this bookmark as private, your bookmark can now be discovered by anyone using the Delicious website.

You also have an automatic list of tags at the far right, which serves as a way to categorize your bookmarks. Unlike bookmarks in a browser, where each bookmark must normally be assigned to a single folder, Delicious makes it possible to add multiple tags to each bookmark, providing you with multiple ways to organize your bookmarks.

If you encourage your friends to use Delicious, or make new friends out of existing Delicious users, you can add any of those individuals to your "network." This gives you a network page where you can view the public bookmarks saved by the people in your network. You can also group your network friends into "bundles" (for instance, a bundle for "genealogists"), so that you can limit your view to just the bookmarks added by those particular individuals.

Another way to see what bookmarks are being added by others for a particular tag is to "subscribe" to that tag. This means that you can see the latest bookmarks that have been given a particular tag. Here's an example for a subscription to the tag "genealogy":

drewsmith's Subscriptions
Bookmarks | Network | Tags | Subscriptions | Inbox

See more bookmarks in Popular or Recent

drewsmith ⟩ Subscriptions   Bookmarks 104721

08 JAN 09 LongLostPeople.com - Find Friends, Family, Lost Loves, Classmates,   3
Adoptions SAVE

⚑ bperritt   GENEALOGY

The Genealogy Guys Podcast SAVED   76

⚑ drewsmith   genealogy   podcast

RootsWeb's WorldConnect Project: Willingham's of Polk County Georgia
SAVE

⚑ hennesstikiodar   family   genealogy   harper   duranko

Subscriptions

▼ All Subscriptions   1

genealogy

▮ Save a new bookmark
⚑ Add a subscription
▸ Subscription options

Finally, there is an RSS button at the bottom of your Subscriptions page, which allows you to add a particular subscription to your collection of RSS-format web feeds. In this way, you can see if new bookmarks have been added to Delicious on topics you are researching without having to visit Delicious itself!

Getting involved with social bookmarking

To get involved with social bookmarking as part of your genealogical research, you might take the following incremental steps:

1. **Search** Delicious for bookmarks of interest.

2. **Create** a free Delicious account.

3. **Upload** existing bookmarks from your browser or add them individually.

4. **Install** a bookmarking tool to make it easier to add bookmarks to Delicious.

5. **Tag** your bookmarks.

6. **Subscribe** to a Delicious tag subscription or to an RSS-format web feed for bookmarks of interest.

Chapter 10:
Sharing personal libraries

Browsing the virtual bookshelves of friends and strangers

Introduction

The real world is full of book clubs, and the online world is no exception. No matter where they are, people enjoy reading books, collecting books, discussing books, sharing books, and wondering what books everyone else is reading, collecting, and discussing. For us genealogists, the local public library's collection of genealogy books may be inadequate to meet all of our particular research needs, and it is not unusual for our home genealogy libraries to consist of hundreds of reference and how-to books.

Because our budgets and home storage are limited, we don't want to buy every possible genealogy book that exists, but we do want to be made aware of new books that can help us with our research. We may want to buy them for ourselves or recommend them for purchase by our local public library. And if all we need is a look-up of a fact or two, we'd be perfectly happy if we knew of someone else who owned the book and who would be willing to look up those facts for us. We need a social networking service built around the books in our personal libraries.

LibraryThing—an overview

The largest and most popular social networking site centered around books is LibraryThing (available online at librarything.com). At this point, nearly 600,000 LibraryThing users have catalogued over 30 million books. As you might have hoped, genealogists have discovered LibraryThing, and the tag "genealogy" has been applied to books in LibraryThing nearly 40,000 times.

LibraryThing provides a vast array of features, including:

- the ability to search for books (held in personal collections by LibraryThing users) by title, author, or descriptive tag, and to see how others have rated and reviewed those books

- the ability to create a personal library catalog that can be accessed from any computer on the Web, and to display and print out lists from the catalog

- the ability to rate and review books and share those ratings and reviews with others, and to talk with others about books

- the ability to discover libraries held by other individuals with common interests

Let's see what happens when we go to LibraryThing's search screen and look for books tagged with "genealogy":

The top portion of the result screen is shown below:

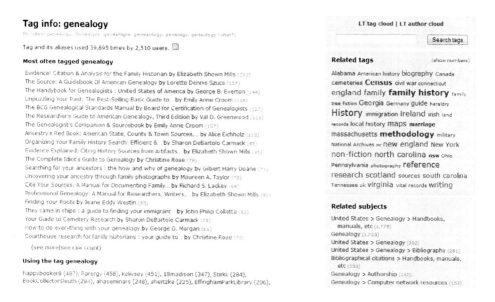

As you can see from the results screen, you learn how many LibraryThing books have been tagged with "genealogy" and by how many different LibraryThing users. You get to see a list, sorted roughly by descending numbers of LibraryThing users, of the books tagged with "genealogy," providing a rough idea of how relatively popular any particular genealogy book is among the LibraryThing community.

Below the list of books is a list of the LibraryThing users most likely to be using the tag "genealogy" (and how many times they have used it). On the right is a "tag cloud," a graphical way to display how often particular tags are used together with the "genealogy" tag. It is no surprise that the tags "family history," "methodology," and "census" are commonly combined with "genealogy" for the same book. Below the tag cloud is a list of catalog subjects arranged in a tree structure, as you might be used to seeing in a public or academic library's catalog. These subjects are related in some way to the tag you've searched for and can be used to further identify books.

Clicking on the title for a particular book provides a lot of details about the book and the people who own copies. Here is the top part of the results screen:

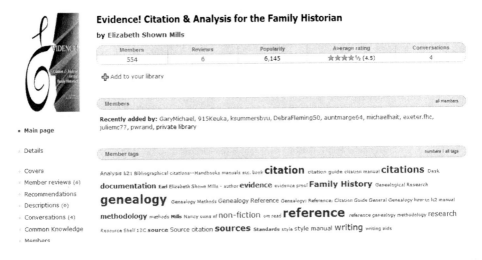

Notice that you can see a list of every LibraryThing member who owns a copy of the book, read reviews and discussions about the book, and use the tag cloud to get a good idea of what topics the book is most likely to cover (as determined by other book owners).

Below the tag cloud is a list of other books that are recommended by LibraryThing's software. These books are usually on the same or closely related topics to the book you were viewing, or are written by the same author:

LibraryThing recommendations

1. Cite Your Sources: A Manual for Documenting Family Histories and Genealogical Records by Richard S. Lackey
2. Quicksheet Citing Online Historical Sources by Elizabeth Shown Mills
3. Evidence Explained: Citing History Sources from Artifacts to Cyberspace by Elizabeth Shown Mills
4. The BCG Genealogical Standards Manual by Board for Certification of Genealogists
5. The Source: A Guidebook Of American Genealogy by Loretto Dennis Szucs
6. Professional Genealogy: A Manual for Researchers, Writers, Editors, Lecturers, and Librarians by Elizabeth Shown Mills
7. Ancestry's Red Book: American State, County & Town Sources, Third Revised Edition by Alice Eichholz
8. The Researcher's Guide to American Genealogy, Third Edition by Val D. Greenwood
9. The Handybook for Genealogists : United States of America by George B. Everton
10. Genealogical Proof Standard: Building a Solid Case by Christine Rose

LibraryThing—putting your own catalog online

Even if you didn't care about what was in anyone else's library, you would find LibraryThing an extremely valuable tool for organizing your home library. How many times have you gone to a genealogy conference, bought a book in the vendor area, and brought it home only to discover that you already owned a copy? (Yes, I know well-known genealogists who have done that.) But the thought of typing in hundreds of titles, authors, and years of publication has prevented you from maintaining a list, and you'd still need some sort of software system to search, sort, categorize, and print your file of books.

LibraryThing allows you to enter up to 200 books free of charge (an unlimited number of books can be entered for a lifetime fee of $25). You can make it so that only you can see what books you have, or you can allow your library catalog to be public.

After you have created a LibraryThing account, edited your profile (if you want other LibraryThing users to know more about you), and decided whether you want your library catalog to be private or public, you're ready to add books in an amazingly painless manner:

Add books to your library

Search

[   ] [Search]

title, author, ISBN, LC card number, etc.

Tags to add

[   ]

Separate with commas, like "history, military history, Napoleon" (**what are tags?**)

Search where?

- Amazon.com (remove)
- Library of Congress (remove)

Or choose from 690 other sources around the world

Other ways to add

Advanced options | add the book manually | import books

Notice above that the fastest and easiest way to add a relatively modern book to your library is to type in the book's ISBN, most often found on the back cover of the book next to the book's bar code. You can also add any number of tags at the same time. Let's add *Evidence Explained* by Elizabeth Shown Mills to our personal library catalog:

Add books to your library

Search

| 9780806317816 | Search |

title, author, ISBN, LC card number, etc.

Tags to add

search elsewhere

Results from Amazon.com (1 result)

Tip: Click the link to add a book to your library.

Evidence Explained: Citing History Sources from Artifacts to Cyberspace by Elizabeth Shown Mills (2007). (more)

LibraryThing goes out to Amazon.com with the ISBN and locates the book cover, title, author, and year of publication. If this is the right book (and it should be unless we mistyped the ISBN), you can click on the title, and the result looks like this:

Add books to your library

Search

| 9780806317816 | Search |

title, author, ISBN, LC card number, etc.

Recently added

Evidence Explained: Citing History Sources from   edit book
Artifacts to Cyberspace by Elizabeth Shown Mills   delete book
228 other members; Tags: None

▶ show quick edit

If this method isn't fast enough for you, there's an advanced option to skip the confirmation so that the book is entered as soon as you type in the ISBN and click the "Search" button.

Clearly, not every book is going to be in Amazon.com, so you may need to perform an additional search using the Library of Congress. In the case of a book with no ISBN, you can search for a book by title or author. And if your book is very rare, you may need to add the descriptive information about your book manually to your library catalog.

Once you have entered a number of books into your library, you can begin to display (and optionally print). Here's the first part of my library so far:

| ≡ List | ▦ Covers | ◇ Tags | | Styles | A | B | C | D | E | ✐ | | ⚡ Power edit | 🖶 Print | | | | | All fiel ▾ | | Search | ❷ |

1 – 20 of 138　　　　　　　　　　　　　　　　　　　next page　　　　　　　　　　　　　　　　[1] 2 3 4 5 6 7

Title ▾	Author	Date	Tags	Publication	Shared
30 Seconds: A Guide to Organizing Your Genealogy Files	Robert R Langrman	2001		Heritage Knights, LLC (2001), Paperback, 82 pages	👤 🖼 ✐ ✕ 14
Abraham's Children: Race, Identity, and the DNA of the Chosen People	Jon Entine	2007	genealogy, DNA	Grand Central Publishing (2007), Hardcover, 432 pages	👤 🖼 ✐ ✕ 28
All Those Wonderful Names: A Potpourri of People, Places, and Things	J. N. Hook	1991		John Wiley & Sons Inc (1991), Paperback, 317 pages	👤 🖼 ✐ ✕ 10
The American Heritage Dictionary of the English Language		2000	reference	Houghton Mifflin (2000), Hardcover, 2076 pages	👥 🖼 ✐ ✕ 1455/19

Double-clicking on any of the fields (Title, Author, Date, Tags, or Publication) allows me to correct errors that may have been introduced during the automatic process of adding the book to my collection. Additional options across the top of the screen allow me to sort my list in different ways, create customized views of my books, or search my library for a particular book.

Getting involved with sharing personal libraries

To get involved with sharing personal libraries as part of your genealogical research, you might take the following incremental steps:

1. **Search** LibraryThing for books of interest.

2. **Create** a free LibraryThing account and enter up to 200 of your books into it.

3. **Subscribe** to an RSS-format web feed for a particular tag so that you can be notified of new books of interest.

4. **Edit** your profile so that others can learn more about you and your interests.

5. **Invite** friends and other genealogical researchers to join LibraryThing and share what's on their shelves.

Chapter 11:
Podcasts

Fireside chats for the 21st Century

podcast (noun): A series of digital audio files available on the Web for listening and downloading, usually resembling a type of radio show; also, a particular episode of a podcast

Introduction

The invention of television didn't kill radio, although it did have a significant impact on the kinds of content found on radio. Not only does radio continue to serve as a major medium for the distribution of music but it also provides news and discussion for people whose eyes may be occupied elsewhere. When you're busy driving a car, exercising, or cleaning the house, your ears are free to listen and learn.

The ability to transmit digital audio over the Web—especially to those networked in by broadband—combined with the development of the portable mp3 player, meant that music and talk could be published on the Web and made available for playing back almost anywhere, from a home computer to a laptop to an mp3 player hooked to a belt. The first Apple iPod was released in 2001, and around the same time, individuals were beginning to experiment with "audioblogging," a way to add audio content to textual blogs. By 2004, the term "podcasting" had taken hold as the term of choice (despite the fact that any kind of mp3 player, not just iPods, could be used to listen to this kind of audio content).

The popularity of podcasting exploded in the last few months of 2004, and while music content predominated among podcast producers and listeners, individuals were exploring new areas of content for special interest groups. Like many other university instructors of the time, I myself began to investigate using podcasting as a way of delivering educational content to my distance learning students. And I began to wonder how long it would be before someone thought about using podcasting as a way to interact with others about genealogical research.

Discovering podcasts about genealogy

Illya D'Addezio's *Genealogy Today* website experimented with podcasting in early 2005, eventually producing a few episodes, but it wouldn't be until the August/September 2005 timeframe before two different genealogy shows began producing a large number of episodes, continuing to the present time: Pat Richley's *DearMYRTLE's Family History Hour*, and my own *Genealogy Guys Podcast*, co-hosted by George G. Morgan (which began as a 30-minute show but expanded to an hour within a few months). At the time of this writing, *DearMYRTLE's Family History Hour* has produced over 70 episodes, while the *Genealogy Guys Podcast* has over 160 episodes available. Other individuals have since begun to produce more specialized podcasts dealing with genealogical technology or researching specific ethnic groups (such as African American, Hispanic, and Irish).

While you can discover podcasts by using Google to search for "genealogy" and "podcasts," a more efficient way is to use a podcast directory. The most popular of these directories is the one available within the iTunes software, which is free for downloading to both Windows and Macintosh systems. If you are a Windows user who does not already have iTunes installed on your system, you can obtain the software by going to itunes.com (which will re-route you to www.apple.com/itunes/overview/). Once you have installed and started the iTunes software, you will see a page like this:

The extremely busy screen is intended to entice you to purchase music and videos from the iTunes Store, but don't worry—the genealogy podcasts we are discussing here are free, and we'll be using the iTunes software only for finding, subscribing to, downloading, and playing podcasts. On the right side of the screen is a "Quick Links" box:

QUICK LINKS

Browse

Power Search

Account

Buy iTunes Gifts

Redeem

Support

My Alerts

Complete My Album

Choose "Power Search" and then choose "Podcasts" from the dropdown "All Results" menu on the left:

Put "genealogy" in the "Description" box, and press the "Search" button:

	▲ Name	Artist	Genre	Price	Popularity
1	Genealogy Gems Podcast - Your Family History ... [CLEAN] ◎	Lisa Louise Cooke	Kids & Family ◎	Free [SUBSCRIBE]	▌▌▌▌▌▌▌
2	The Genealogy Guys Podcast ◎	George G. Morgan & Drew Smith	Kids & Family ◎	Free [SUBSCRIBE]	▌▌▌▌▌▌▌
3	Family Roots Radio Genealogy Hour [CLEAN] ◎	Kory L. Meyerink	History ◎	Free [SUBSCRIBE]	▌▌▌▌▌
4	Eastman's Online Genealogy Newsletter ◎	Dick Eastman	Kids & Family ◎	Free [SUBSCRIBE]	▌▌▌
5	Family History: Genealogy Made Easy ◎	Lisa Louise Cooke ◎	Kids & Family ◎	Free [SUBSCRIBE]	▌▌▌▌▌▌
6	Irish Roots Cafe Genealogy and History ◎	Michael O'Laughlin ◎	History ◎	Free [SUBSCRIBE]	▌▌▌▌▌
7	Family History Minute ◎	Brian Mickelson (FHM Podcaster)	Education ◎	Free [SUBSCRIBE]	▌▌▌
8	Genealogy On Demand ◎	Shamele Jordon	Training ◎	Free [SUBSCRIBE]	▌▌▌
9	Family Tree Magazine Podcast ◎	Family Tree Magazine	Kids & Family ◎	Free [SUBSCRIBE]	▌▌▌
10	DearMYRTLE's Family History Hour ◎	DearMYRTLE	Society & Culture ◎	Free [SUBSCRIBE]	▌▌▌
11	Family History Podcast [CLEAN] ▯ ◎	Will Howells	Hobbies ◎	Free [SUBSCRIBE]	▌▌▌
12	Tracing Your Roots ◎	BBC Radio 4 ◎	History ◎	Free [SUBSCRIBE]	▌▌▌
13	Irish in America: History and Genealogy ◎	Michael O'Laughlin ◎	History ◎	Free [SUBSCRIBE]	▌▌
14	Under the Tree - African-American History [CLEAN] ◎	Meredith Williams	History ◎	Free [SUBSCRIBE]	▌▌
15	Irish Song and Recitation: History, Chat and Sing ◎	Michael O'Laughlin ◎	Music ◎	Free [SUBSCRIBE]	▌▌
16	Nuestra Familia Unida: History and Genealogy -... [CLEAN] ◎	Joseph Puentes	History ◎	Free [SUBSCRIBE]	▌▌
17	Irish Roots Cafe Videos: History and Genealogy ▯ ◎	Michael O'Laughlin ◎	History ◎	Free [SUBSCRIBE]	▌
18	Federation of Genealogical Societies 2008 Phily Podcast ◎	Shamele Jordon	Kids & Family ◎	Free [SUBSCRIBE]	▌
19	Enhanced Irish Families Worldwide: History and Genealogy ◎	Michael O'Laughlin ◎	History ◎	Free [SUBSCRIBE]	▌
20	Family History Expos Genealogy Podcast [CLEAN] ◎	Family History Expos.com	Educational Tech... ◎	Free [SUBSCRIBE]	▌

Although there are other podcast directories available on the Web (and the others do not require any specialized software to download and use), the directory in iTunes remains one of the most comprehensive podcast directories and the best place to discover new genealogy podcasts.

Subscribing to and downloading podcasts

A major advantage of using the iTunes software to discover podcasts of interest is that the same software can be used to subscribe to, download, and play back podcasts. Over 50% of the listeners to the *Genealogy Guys Podcast* use iTunes to download our episodes each week. (Almost all of our remaining listeners go directly to our website and download episodes individually.) You'll notice that each podcast in the list has a "Subscribe" button, which will add the particular podcast to the list of podcasts automatically downloaded by iTunes when new episodes become available:

Clicking the "Subscribe" button begins the download process for the latest episode:

Kind	Name	Status	
🎙	The Genealogy Guys Podcast #161 - 2009 January 5 / The Genealogy Guys Podcast [CLEAN]	16.4 MB of 25.4 MB - 21 seconds remaining	⊘

You can also display a list of all past episodes, and then pick and choose any that you'd like to download and add to your iTunes library:

◀Artwor	▲	Podcast		Time	Release Da	Description	
		▼ The Genealogy Guys Po... (GET ALL)			1/6/2009	Genealogy Chat with George G. Morgan and Drew Smith	ⓘ
♫		The Genealogy Guys ... [CLEAN]		55:20	1/6/2009	This week's news includes: Ancestry.com launches a new Florida State Census Collection (1867, 1875, 1...	ⓘ
		The Genealog... [CLEAN] (GET)			12/26/2008	The Guys wish all their listeners a wonderful holiday season!This week's news includes: The North Carol...	ⓘ
		The Genealog... [CLEAN] (GET)			12/16/2008	This week's news includes: Allen Weinstein, Archivist of the United States, submitted his resignation to t...	ⓘ
		The Genealog... [CLEAN] (GET)			12/8/2008	We have a new microphone cable for the mixer this week, and we hope that alleviates the stereo cut ou...	ⓘ
		The Genealog... [CLEAN] (GET)			11/30/2008	We apologize for the few cut-outs of stereo in this week's episode. We have replaced a damaged cable...	ⓘ
		The Genealog... [CLEAN] (GET)			11/13/2008	This week's news includes: Sirius Innovations introduces a new genealogy website at http://www.siriusg...	ⓘ
		The Genealogy Guys P... (GET)			11/5/2008	This week's news includes: Ancestry.com launches the world's largest collection of Jewish documents; th...	ⓘ
		The Genealog... [CLEAN] (GET)			10/26/2008	This week's news includes: Ancestry.com has renamed its self-publishing tool from AncestryPress to MyC...	ⓘ
		The Genealog... [CLEAN] (GET)			10/13/2008	This week's news includes: Art Lacagnie, founder of The Gold Bug (producer of AniMap software), died o...	ⓘ
		The Genealog... [CLEAN] (GET)			9/29/2008	While George relaxes on a cruise ship off the Pacific coast of Mexico (ok, so he's doing some genealogy l...	ⓘ
		The Genealog... [CLEAN] (GET)			9/17/2008	This week's news includes: The Association of Professional Genealogists (APG) recognized genealogists ...	ⓘ
		The Genealog... [CLEAN] (GET)			9/9/2008	CELEBRATING OUR 150TH EPISODE!The Guys are celebrating the 150th episode of the podcast which b...	ⓘ
		The Genealog... [CLEAN] (GET)			8/31/2008	A correction to last week's story about the death of a Confederate widow can be found in last week's sh...	ⓘ
		The Genealog... [CLEAN] (GET)			8/23/2008	This week's news includes: Alberta Martin (Oops, correction, this should have been Maudie Hopkins), 93,...	ⓘ
		The Genealog... [CLEAN] (GET)			8/15/2008	This episode is dedicated to our dear friend, Tom Ryder, who passed away today in Port Charlotte, Flori...	ⓘ
		The Genealog... [CLEAN] (GET)			8/5/2008	This week's news includes: archaeologists are actively working to locate the identities of everyone interr...	ⓘ
		The Genealog... [CLEAN] (GET)			7/26/2008	This week's news includes: FamilySearch and Ancestry.com team up to publish new images and enhance ...	ⓘ
		The Genealog... [CLEAN] (GET)			7/19/2008	This week's news includes: Abraham Lincoln's ancestry is questioned; Ancestry.com announces new dat...	ⓘ
		The Genealog... [CLEAN] (GET)			7/9/2008	This week's news includes: George Washington's boyhood home is found; and new features are unveiled...	ⓘ
		The Genealog... [CLEAN] (GET)			6/22/2008	This week's news includes: the new Midwest Genealogy Center in Independence, Missouri, opened on 2...	ⓘ
		The Genealogy Guys P... (GET)			6/15/2008	This week's news includes: Ancestry.com announces the doubling of its digitized newspaper collection; a...	ⓘ
		The Genealogy Guys P... (GET)			6/5/2008	This week's news includes: Genclass.com (http://genclass.com/) partners with Familylink.com (http:...	ⓘ
		The Genealog... [CLEAN] (GET)			5/30/2008	The news this week includes: a new series at RootsTelevision.com titled Unclaimed Persons which the pr...	ⓘ
		The Genealog... [CLEAN] (GET)			5/22/2008	News this week includes: FamilySearch teams with FamilyLink.com to bring online the Brenner Collection ...	ⓘ
		The Genealog... [CLEAN] (GET)			5/15/2008	This week's news includes: Geni, Inc. (geni.com) announces the new functional availability for users to u...	ⓘ
		The Genealog... [CLEAN] (GET)			5/9/2008	This week's news includes: the Vatican has issued a letter instructing all dioceses not to give any informa...	ⓘ
		The Genealog... [CLEAN] (GET)			5/1/2008	News this week includes: Geni.com (http://www.geni.com/) announces new features, including a family...	ⓘ
		The Genealog... [CLEAN] (GET)			4/23/2008	In the News, The Guys review two new publications: <span style="font-weight: bold;"> <span style="F...	ⓘ
		The Genealog... [CLEAN] (GET)			4/16/2008	This week's news includes the following: Ancestry.com launches the Drouin Collection of 29 million Frenc...	ⓘ
		The Genealog... [CLEAN] (GET)			4/1/2008	Drew addresses proving relationships using mitochondrial DNA. He then discusses two genealogical book...	ⓘ
		The Genealog... [CLEAN] (GET)			3/25/2008	This week's news includes: NBC has purchased rights to create an American version of the popular BBC ...	ⓘ
		The Genealog... [CLEAN] (GET)			3/18/2008	In this week's news: NARA (http://www.archives.gov) posts free passenger lists online, including Russi...	ⓘ
		The Genealog... [CLEAN] (GET)			3/11/2008	George delivers a lot of news this week: the New England Historic and Genealogical Society (http://www...	ⓘ
		The Genealog... [CLEAN] (GET)			3/4/2008	This week's news includes: condolences to the family of Chuck Knuthson, a great genealogical speaker, r...	ⓘ

Any episodes that you have downloaded into your iTunes library can now be transferred to an mp3 player. But you don't need an mp3 player to listen to a podcast. You can use the player features of iTunes to play the episode on your computer. (And if you're not using iTunes to download and play the episodes, you can still download them manually directly from the podcast website and play them using your computer's standard media player, such as Windows Media Player.)

Interacting with genealogy podcasters

Because each podcast has its own website, you can go there to view details about each episode, learn about the podcasters themselves, and discover ways to contact the podcasters with your own questions and ideas (which may be used on future episodes):

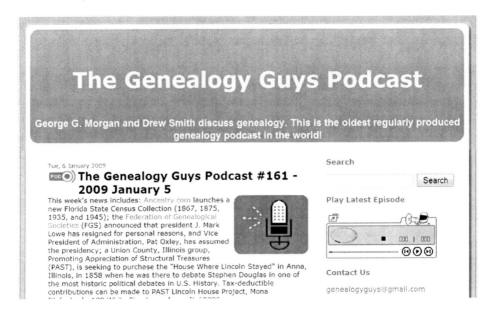

The "Search" box on the top right allows you to search the descriptions of past episodes to find particular episodes of interest, and the player on the right lets you immediately play the most recent episode or work backwards through past episodes. The "show notes" (the descriptions for each episode) also provide active links to content discussed during the episode.

Further down the page on the right-hand side is an RSS button that allows you to subscribe to podcast episodes using your standard feed reader (such as Google Reader). This lets you learn about new episodes without using iTunes or some other specialized podcast tool, and you can then go from Google Reader to the episode itself in order to play it.

Getting involved with podcasts

To get involved with podcasts as part of your genealogical research, you might take the following incremental steps:

1. **Search** iTunes or another podcast directory for podcasts of interest.

2. **Visit** a podcast site in order to listen to or download an episode.

3. **Subscribe** to a podcast using an RSS-format web feed (with the help of iTunes or Google Reader).

Chapter 12:
Social networking for its own sake

Keeping up with friends and family

Introduction

In previous chapters of this book, we have looked at online services that focus on such things as genealogical queries (mailing lists and message boards), textual documents (blogs, wikis, and collaborative editing), photos and videos, browser bookmarks, books, and audio files (podcasts). But does social networking have to be "about" anything at all? Can it simply be about keeping in touch with friends, family, and colleagues?

If you asked the average computer user what "social networking" is about, they'd probably mention Facebook. Facebook is not the only "generic" social networking site; the first of that type may have been Friendster, and MySpace remains a very popular site (especially among younger users) with over 100 million accounts. Classmates.com continues to connect individuals who graduated together from a specific high school or college, and LinkedIn aims for a more professional type of networking. But Facebook may have become the social networking site of choice for genealogists, and for some interesting reasons. Let's take a closer look.

Getting started with Facebook and editing your profile

When you go to Facebook (online at facebook.com) for the first time, you can quickly and easily create a free account. After that, during future visits, you can have Facebook automatically log you in:

Once you have an account, your first action will likely be to edit and develop your personal profile. You will need to decide how much information you want to share about yourself, keeping in mind any privacy concerns you might have. As you acquire friends on Facebook, they will be able to see this information. Here's a sample:

If you want people to know even more about you than the "basics," you can add many additional details. Facebook provides some prompts to help you with this:

▼ **Personal Information**

Activities:

Interests:

genealogy

Favorite Music:

Favorite TV Shows:

Favorite Movies:

Favorite Books:

Favorite Quotations:

Want to make sure that other people can reach you? You can provide as much contact information as you like:

▼ **Contact Information**

Emails: amsmith@lib.usf.edu   🔒
                drewsmithtpa@gmail.com   🔒
                Add / Remove Emails

IM Screen Name(s):   drewsmithtpa   Google Talk ▼   🔒
                     Add another screen name

Mobile Phone: 813.263.2028   🔒
Land Phone: 🔒
School Mailbox: LIB122   🔒
Residence:
Room: 🔒

Address: 15611 Jericho Dr   🔒
City/Town: Odessa, FL
Zip: 33556-3016

Website: 🔒

                [Save Changes]   [Cancel]

    If you want former classmates to find you or want others to know
about your educational credentials all the way back to high school, there's
lots of room for that:

▼ **Education and Work**

College/University:	University of South Florida	1995 ▼
	Attended for Graduate School ▼	
Concentration:		
	Add Another Concentration	
Degree:	Library and Information Science	
	Remove School	

College/University:	Clemson	1987 ▼
	Attended for Graduate School ▼	
Concentration:		
	Add Another Concentration	
Degree:	Industrial Management	
	Remove School	

College/University:	Clemson	1978 ▼
	Attended for College ▼	
Concentration:	Electrical Engineering	
	Add Another Concentration	
	Remove School	

Add Another School

High School:	Newberry High School	1974 ▼
	Remove High School	

Add Another High School

And if you want former co-workers to find you or others to know about your work history, there's plenty of space for that too:

Employer:	USF Library
Position:	Information Literacy Librarian
Description:	
City/Town:	Tampa, FL
Time Period:	☑ I currently work here.
	February ▾ 2007 ▾ to present.
	Remove Job

Employer:	USF School of Library and Infor
Position:	Instructor
Description:		
City/Town:	Tampa, FL
Time Period:	☐ I currently work here.
	August ▾ 1994 ▾ to February ▾ 2007 ▾
	Remove Job

Employer:	University of South Florida - Scl
Position:	Graduate Assistant
Description:	
City/Town:	Tampa, FL
Time Period:	☐ I currently work here.

The point of showing you these screens is to give you an idea of how extensive the tools to talk about yourself are, but always keep in mind that you are free to leave blank any screen you like. There is no requirement that you share any of this information with anyone else. However, these details may provide a way for long-lost friends, family members, and co-workers to find you and distinguish you from other people with the same name.

Photos, status lines, walls, and other ways to share information

Because Facebook provides so many ways to share information with others, we can only scratch the surface in this chapter. But here are some of my favorites, beginning with photos:

Once you are in Facebook, your friends can tag any photos they find containing your image, and all of these photos can be viewed together on your own page. You can certainly upload your own photos (and those of friends), and tag anyone else's photos if you find yourself or friends in them. Each photo can be accompanied by comments.

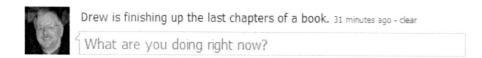

At the top of your Facebook page is a place for you to keep others aware of what you are doing (as often as you like). Each time that you change your status, your friends will be able to see the change on their own pages (in their "News Feed"). Some individuals go months without changing their status, while others may update it several times a day. Speaking of your "News Feed," you will also be notified when your friends add new photos, attend events, are tagged in photos, join groups, change their relationship status, or acquire new friends of their own. If you choose, you can have these notifications sent to you via e-mail (in case you don't visit Facebook very often).

You can also communicate privately or publicly with other Facebook users. The most public way is to write on a person's "Wall." You have a lot of options in this area:

| Wall | Info | Photos | Boxes | Notes | Books | » | + |

🧑 **Update Status** 🔗 **Share Link** 🖼 **Add Photos** 📹 **Add Video** 📄 **Write Note** ▾

Title:	
Body:	
In this note:	
Privacy:	🔒 Who can see this?
	My Networks and Friends ▾

Everyone
My Networks and Friends
People at USF and Friends
Friends of Friends
Only Friends
Customize...

Add ...

Post

All Posts · Posts by Drew · Posts by Others · ⚙ Settings

Groups for genealogists

Facebook users can create and join groups, which are areas of Facebook that allow members to post messages, upload photos, and interact about areas of common interest:

My Groups | Browse Groups   Help

👥 **Groups**   Search for Groups   (+ **Create a New Group**)

Once you have joined one or more groups, you can see the status of your groups (from most active to least active):

And if you're wondering how many genealogy-related groups there already are on Facebook, this may give you some idea:

With over 500 groups to choose from, it may be difficult to decide where to start. But let's look at one of my personal favorites, Unclaimed Persons. When you first visit the Unclaimed Persons group, you'll see this:

Unclaimed Persons
Global

Basic Info
Type: Organizations - Advocacy Organizations
Description: It's a quiet but disturbing epidemic. Bodies are piling up in morgues with no family to claim them. Coroners are turning to an unexpected resource for help. Can genealogy and genealogists help solve these Unclaimed Persons cases?

New volunteers, please visit our website http://www.unclaimedpersons.org to learn more.

483 volunteers as of January 17, 2009. Thank you all!

See http://www.rootstelevision.com/players/player_conferences.php?bctid=17 82539533 to watch an interview with one of the Unclaimed Persons founders (first half of the video).

Contact Info
Email: unclaimedpersons@rootstelevision.com
Website: http://unclaimedpersons.org
Location: Provo, UT

Members
Displaying 8 of 485 members   See All

View Discussion Board
Invite People to Join
Leave Group

Share +

Officers

Unclaimed Persons
Founder
Megan Smolenyak Smolenyak
(Philadelphia, PA)
Founder
Marcy Brown (Provo, UT)
Founder

This particular group has a very active discussion board, where volunteer genealogists do research on specific deceased individuals, sharing information and attempting to locate the deceased's next-of-kin. At the time of this writing, 34 cases have been solved.

Getting involved with Facebook

To get involved with Facebook as part of your genealogical research, you might take the following incremental steps:

1. **Create** a free Facebook account.

2. **Upload** photos and modify your profile to share information about yourself with others.

3. **Search** for people you know on Facebook and invite them to become your Facebook friends.

4. **Join** groups of interest.

5. **Participate** in the Unclaimed Persons group.

Chapter 13:
Virtual worlds

Meet your genealogy friends in 3-D

virtual world (noun): A computer-generated environment intended to simulate some aspect of a real-world environment, usually represented in three dimensions

avatar (noun): A personal representation of the computer user within the computer-generated environment, often appearing as a relatively realistic human likeness

prim (noun): A fundamental geometric shape (such as a cube or sphere) used within the Second Life system to construct complex landscapes, buildings, other objects, and avatars

rez (verb): To cause an object to appear within Second Life

Introduction

Attempting to explain three-dimensional virtual worlds within the pages of a book to those who have never used them is a bit like attempting to explain TV or movies to people who have never experienced them. (This doesn't mean that I'm not going to try; it just means that the two-dimensional book you're holding is an inadequate substitute for a three-dimensional experience.)

If you've ever played a video game (or watched a member of your family play one), you have some idea of what it is like to immerse yourself in another world, where you may feel that you are seeing and interacting with another landscape, even to the point of "walking around" and "holding" and "dropping" things. Do this frequently enough or for long enough periods of time, especially within an increasingly realistic simulated environment, and you may occasionally forget that you are a real body sitting in front of a computer, pressing buttons and typing text. Now combine this type of experience with an international computer network, meaning that you are sharing the same virtual space with many thousands of other individuals at the same time, and the resulting complexity may give you the strange sensation of actually being in another place with lots of other people. (And some of those other people may be genealogists! But let's not get ahead of ourselves.)

Online virtual worlds have been around for years, and some of them have gotten a great deal of publicity, especially World of Warcraft, which came online in late 2004. As a result of World of Warcraft and similar online services, the casual user may consider virtual worlds to be nothing but complex video games in which the goal is to kill or destroy things (or other players). But even before World of Warcraft came into existence, computer programmers were developing virtual environments in which there were no specific goals, no "winning" and "losing," and no accumulation of "points." Instead, the purpose of many of these virtual world environments was simply to be creative and interact with other users, much as the Web itself had done since the early 1990s in a more two-dimensional form.

In 2003, a company known as Linden Lab released Second Life; today, millions of individuals have created Second Life accounts, and at any given moment, tens of thousands of individuals around the world are visiting Second Life and interacting with its virtual environment and with each other.

Getting started with Second Life

Unlike many of the other forms of social networking discussed in this book, Second Life requires sufficiently powerful computer hardware and specialized software in order to work. After all, in order to create the illusion of an ever-changing three-dimensional environment on your computer's screen, your computer must have a sufficiently fast (broadband) Internet connection and CPU, must have sufficient memory, and must possess a sufficiently powerful computer graphics card. Detailed minimum and recommended requirements can be found here: secondlife.com/support/sysreqs.php.

If your computer system meets the minimum requirements, you can proceed to download and install the free Second Life client software. During the process of installing the software and accessing the Second Life servers for the first time, you will need to create your free Second Life account, which is identified by your "avatar" (Second Life user) name. Because this name cannot be changed later, I recommend that you give some careful thought as to what name you will be using in Second Life. The avatar name, like a real name in most Western cultures, consists of a "first" name and a "last" name. You have a great deal of discretion as to your first name, and some individuals use their real first name or some variation of it. Your avatar's last name is normally chosen from a drop-down box of pre-approved Second Life surnames, although the list of such names appears to change from time to time. For instance, my avatar's name is "Drew Rodinia." When you log in to Second Life using the Second Life software, you will be entering your avatar name and your chosen password:

Because Linden Lab is headquartered in San Francisco and because it is convenient for all Second Life users around the world to share a common time reference, "Second Life Time" (SLT) is the same as Pacific Time. This is important to know if you're planning to meet a friend in Second Life or attend a publicized Second Life event.

When you first create your Second Life avatar (the way in which you will be represented within Second Life), you will choose whether to be male or female, and you will then be given a variety of physical options, which you can customize in countless ways (height, weight, skin color, hair color, eye color, etc.). You are free to change your appearance later, as often as you like. You can also alter your basic set of clothing, and during your time in Second Life, you will be able to acquire additional outfits to customize your appearance.

As with many other social networking services, your Second Life account has an associated public profile, which you can edit as you see fit:

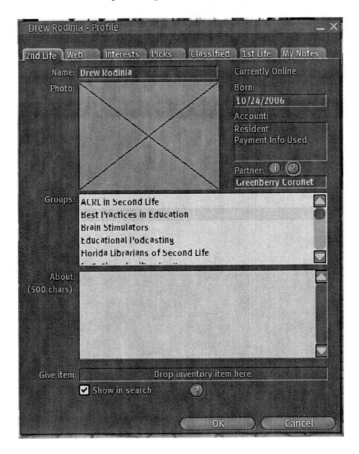

Note that your Second Life "birthdate" is the date you first joined Second Life. The remaining tabs allow you to specify your interests to others, identify your favorite places in Second Life, and tell about who you are in "1st Life" (real life), if you so choose. You can include a real photo of yourself or any other photo you like (even a photo of your avatar's face). The "My Notes" tab is especially useful for keeping track of other avatars. For instance, when you click on another user's avatar, you can edit the "My Notes" tab for that avatar (you are the only one who sees it) and enter information about them (such as their real name if they have told it to you).

To be honest, using Second Life involves a significant learning curve beyond nearly all other social networking tools. In a sense, you'll need to learn how to move around within the environment and how to communicate with other users. Fortunately, new Second Life users are automatically taken to a tutorial area where they can practice altering their appearance, moving around, and communicating. It should be noted that Second Life users have many different ways to communicate with others, including private text messages to an individual or group, text messages that can be read by anyone in the vicinity of the avatar, and real-time voice communication (preferably using a headset).

Genealogy on Second Life

Like the World Wide Web itself, Second Life is a very large environment connecting millions of users, but there are a few specific areas set aside for genealogists, as well as groups you can join in order to be notified of genealogy-related events. Just as the Web is divided into interconnected websites, Second Life is divided into interconnected islands, each of which can be further subdivided into parcels of land on which individuals and groups have constructed buildings and other interactive spaces. Here is the Genealogy Research Center, a kind of public genealogy library located on Info Island (a space maintained by librarians around the world):

The contents of the Genealogy Research Center are determined by a group of volunteers and are changed from time to time to reflect different aspects of genealogical research (at the time of this writing, much of the content on the first floor is designed to explain the basics of using DNA for genealogical research, while the second floor is an exhibit related to online census information). The GRC contains interactive wall displays, places to sit and chat with other Second Life users, and exhibits that can be used to link to other resources on the Web.

Another genealogy-specific area within Second Life is Just Genealogy (sponsored by Heritage Books) on the island of Wollah. Here you will find a calendar of genealogy-related events, often taught by avatar Clarise Beaumont:

Second Life is a fun way of making new friends from around the world (the largest group of users are from outside the United States), practicing foreign languages, exploring beautiful and unusual landscapes, engaging with educational and cultural exhibits, and tapping into your creative side as you alter your appearance or build objects that others can see and use. You may find it entertaining and educational to give it a try.

Getting involved with Second Life

To get involved with Second Life as part of your genealogical research, you might take the following incremental steps:

1. **Create** a free Second Life account and download and install the software.

2. **Modify** your avatar and edit your profile.

3. **Visit** genealogy-related sites on Second Life and participate in genealogy events.

4. **Join** a Second Life genealogy group.

Chapter 14:
Genealogy-specific social networking

Sites designed just for us genealogists

Introduction

The tools previously described in this book were not designed specifically for genealogists, nor are they currently used primarily by genealogists. Message boards, mailing lists, blogs, wikis, collaborative editing tools, photo and video sharing sites, social bookmarking sites, library sharing sites, podcasts, Facebook-style sites, and Second Life were created with no particular kind of user in mind, and as such they are not tailored to the special needs of genealogists.

But genealogists have the unique need to record and share information about their families, locate long-lost relatives, discover new cousins, and collaborate with other genealogical researchers. As early as 1998, My Family.com, a service currently owned by The Generations Network, was set up to allow families to share a common site, although it did not include all of the communication and searching features we now find in modern social networking sites. In the past few years, a large number of new genealogy-oriented social networking sites have come into existence, and it would be impossible to discuss all of them in detail. Among the most popular are the following:

- Geni, based in the United States

- Dynastree (formerly known as ItsOurTree), based in Germany and used throughout Europe

- MyHeritage, based in Israel with users in the United States and Europe

In this chapter, I'll use Geni as the representative example of this kind of social networking site.

Getting started with Geni

Creating your free Geni account is as simple as navigating to geni .com and entering your name, e-mail address, and gender. You can then name your family site and either begin to add family members individually or upload a GEDCOM-format file that you had previously created with genealogy software or downloaded from another online service. Note that it is not currently possible to upload a GEDCOM-format file directly into an existing family file, although there are ways to create two different family files and merge them. So it is recommended that you either begin with an existing GEDCOM-format file or create your family tree from scratch by entering names one at a time.

When you log in to Geni, you'll see your personal home page:

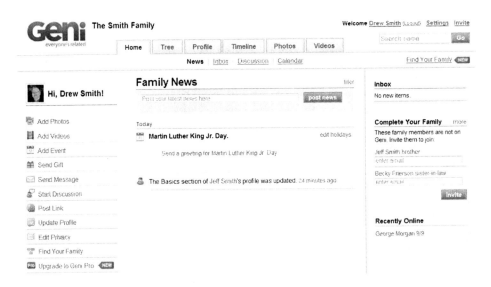

Notice that as you add living family members to your tree, you will have the option of providing e-mail addresses for them if you would like to have them automatically invited to access your information on Geni. If you have already been using other generic social networking sites, you will recognize many of Geni's features, such as photo and video sharing, an area for sending and receiving messages, a place to engage in a message-board-style discussion, and an area to create and update a detailed personal profile. In this chapter, we'll focus on features unique to a genealogy-oriented site.

In order to make it easier to add living family members to your site, you can have Geni "Find Your Family." This means that Geni will go through your e-mail software's address book to identify the names and addresses of family members and, at your request, send them invitations to join Geni. This works for a number of popular e-mail systems such as Gmail, Hotmail, and Yahoo.

Find Your Family

The easiest way to find family members on Geni is to search your address book:

Your Email: **drewsmithtpa@gmail.com**   change address book

Email Password: ••••••

- Geni will not store your password or contact information
- Geni will never email anyone without your direct consent

Next » or Skip

Geni will then list everyone in your e-mail software's address book, beginning with people who share the same surname as individuals already in your family tree. You then have the option of indicating how each individual is related to you (if they are) and choosing which of them should get an invitation to Geni.

Once you have identified which individuals in your address book are relatives (you can also skip this step), you can then identify which remaining individuals are friends. This automated process allows you to quickly add living relatives and other genealogy collaborators to your site.

Working with your family tree

The "Tree" tab provides the area that allows you to add individuals and manipulate your family tree. Here is a basic family tree with five individuals entered so far:

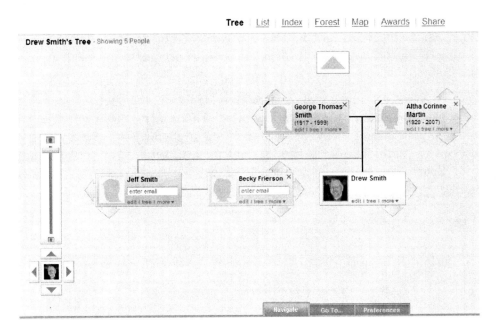

As the number of individuals in your tree increases, you can use the slider on the left to zoom out from your tree, and you can use the arrows on the bottom left to move around the tree. You can also click on the tree's image and drag it around to view nearby parts of the tree.

By clicking on the name of an individual, you can view his personal profile and provide additional details (such as birth date/location, marriage date/location, etc.), add photos and videos, share stories about him, and so forth. The arrows that point up from an individual allow you to add parents, the arrows pointing to the side allow you to add siblings and spouses/partners, and the arrows pointing down allow you to add children. For all individuals, you can choose a display name (such as the name or nickname they were commonly known by in life) but also preserve their full birth name (including the maiden name for a woman) in their profile.

In List view, you can see the names of everyone in your file (or just a subset):

List of Drew Smith's Family

Showing 1-5 of 5 people in: [My Family ▾]   ☑ include deceased

Sort by:	First Name	L	My Family	Relation	Added By	Immediate Family	Action
		My Tree				

		Relation	Added By	Immediate Family	Action
[photo]	Drew Smith "Drew" Citrus Park, Fld	My Tree / My Blood Relatives / My Inlaws / My Ancestors / My Descendants	yourself	Me	Son of Altha Corinne and George Thomas Smith Brother of Jeff Smith	View Tree View List
	Altha Corinne	Recently Added / Recently Joined / Recently Modified	Andrew's mother	Me	Wife of George Thomas Smith Mother of Jeff Smith and Me	View Tree View List Remove from Family Group
	George Thomas Smith (1937–1999)	Invited By Me / Added By Me	Andrew's father	Me	Husband of Altha Corinne Father of Jeff Smith and Me	View Tree View List Remove from Family Group
	Jeff Smith (invite)		Andrew's brother	Me	Son of Altha Corinne and George Thomas Smith Husband of Becky Frierson Brother of Me	View Tree View List Remove from Family Group
	Becky Frierson (invite)		Andrew's sister-in-law	Me	Wife of Jeff Smith	View Tree View List Remove from Family Group

Index view gives you a quick way to locate individuals in your tree by surname:

Index of Last Names in Drew Smith's Family

Showing 5 people with 3 last names

F   Frierson 1

M   Martin 1

S   Smith 3

As your in-laws begin to create their own trees within Geni, you'll be able to link your tree to theirs as a kind of "forest":

Your Forest

Your tree is not connected to any other trees by marriage. Add more relatives to your tree to connect to other trees.

Tree Name	Connected By Marriage To	Size	
Drew Smith's Tree		5	Actions ⌄

Map view allows you to display a world map with a choice of either current locations of relatives or birth locations:

Map of Drew Smith's Family and Friends

Showing 1 out of 6 people mapped by: ◉ current location ◎ place of birth

It should be noted that Geni provides a large number of settings for privacy access, as well as for navigating the family tree.

Finally, it should be noted that Geni can be searched for specific full names or surnames, so that you can locate possible distant relatives who are already using Geni. Note that you will probably be limited as to how much information you can view about other individuals until you are added as a family member or friend by the person who posted his family's information.

Getting involved with genealogy-specific social networking sites

To get involved with genealogy-specific social networking sites as part of your genealogical research, you might take the following incremental steps:

1.   **Create** a free account on Geni.

2.   **Edit** your personal profile in order to let distant relatives and other researchers know more about you, adding events to your personal timeline.

3. **Upload** an existing GEDCOM-format file or manually enter individuals into your site so that they can be discovered by others.

4. **Upload** family photos and videos to your site.

5. **Add** family news to your site.

6. **Search** for names in the family trees of others.

7. **Communicate** with other users by sending them messages or inviting them to your family group.

8. **Discuss** topics in your site's message area with other family members.